Health Science Projects About Nutrition

Robert Gardner

Science Projects

Enslow Publishers, Inc.

40 Industrial Road   PO Box 38
Box 398   Aldershot
Berkeley Heights, NJ 07922   Hants GU12 6BP
USA   UK

http://www.enslow.com

Library of Congress Cataloging-in-Publication Data

Gardner, Robert, 1929–
     Health science projects about nutrition / Robert Gardner.
        p. cm. — (Science projects)
     Includes bibliographical references and index.
     ISBN 0-7660-1442-8
     1. Nutrition—Experiments—Juvenile literature. [1. Nutrition—Experiments.
    2. Experiments.] I. Title.
     QP143. G37 2002
     612.3'9'078—dc21

                                  2001000306

Printed in the United States of America

10 9 8 7 6 5 4 3 2 1

To Our Readers:
We have done our best to make sure all Internet Addresses in this book were active and
appropriate when we went to press. However, the author and the publisher have no control
over and assume no liability for the material available on those Internet sites or on other
Web sites they may link to. Any comments or suggestions can be sent by e-mail to
comments@enslow.com or to the address on the back cover.

Illustration credits: Stephen F. Delisle, pp. 16, 19, 24, 27, 29, 36, 40, 59, 67, 77,
87; Enslow Publishers, Inc., p. 101.

Cover illustration: Jerry McCrea (foreground); © Corel Corporation
(background).

Contents

*appropriate ideas for science fair project

*appropriate ideas for science fair project

Introduction

The science projects and experiments in this book involve weight, food, and nutrition. You can gain weight by eating lots of food. To lose weight you must eat less food than is needed to meet the energy you use in carrying out your daily activities. But these activities include processes you might not regard as action. For example, even when you are sleeping, chemical activity is taking place in your body to provide the heat required to keep your body temperature at a normal level of approximately 37°C (98.6°F).

The food you eat provides the energy you need to stay active as well as warm. That food should also be nutritious. It should provide the minerals and vitamins you need as well as the energy found in the three basic types of food—carbohydrates, proteins, and fats.

To obtain data for some of the projects in this book you will have to talk to members of your family, especially those who prepare the meals you eat. In some projects you may need people to help you with experiments, because more than one pair of hands will be required. Since some of the experiments can take a significant amount of time, try to choose friends who are patient as well as interested. It would be best if you can work with people who enjoy experimenting as much as you do.

Like all good scientists, you will find it useful to record in a notebook your ideas, notes, data, and anything you can conclude from your experiments. That way, you can keep track of the information you gather and the conclusions you reach. Using your notebook, you can refer to past experiments, which may help you in doing future projects. In some of the experiments, you will have to make some calculations. Therefore, you may find it helpful to have a calculator nearby as you do these experiments and analyze the data you collect.

Science Fairs

Some of the projects in this book might be appropriate for a science fair. Those projects are indicated with an asterisk (*). However, judges at science fairs do not reward projects or experiments that are simply copied from a book. For example, a model of a cell, which is commonly found at these fairs, would probably not impress judges unless it was done in a novel or creative way. A model of a cell that would undergo cell division or demonstrate osmosis while judges watched would receive more consideration than a rigid papier-mâché model.

Science fair judges seek to reward creative thought and imagination. However, it is difficult to be creative or imaginative unless you are really interested in your project. Therefore, choose something that appeals to you. Consider, too, your ability and the cost of materials needed for the project.

If you decide to use a project found in this book for a science fair, you will need to find ways to modify or extend it. This should not be difficult because, as you do these projects, new ideas for experiments will come to mind. These new experiments will make excellent science fair projects because they spring from your own mind and are interesting to you.

If you decide to enter a science fair and have never done so before, you should read some of the books listed in the bibliography, including *Science Fair Projects—Planning, Presenting, Succeeding*, which is one of the books in this series. These books deal specifically with science fairs and will provide plenty of helpful hints and lots of useful information that will enable you to avoid the pitfalls that sometimes plague first-time entrants. You will learn how to prepare appealing reports that include charts and graphs, how to set up and display your work, how to present your project, and how to relate to judges and visitors.

Safety First

Most of the projects included in this book are perfectly safe. However, some of them involve the use of dangerous chemicals and heat. In these instances you will be reminded to work with a responsible adult. The following safety rules are also well worth reading before you start any project.

1. Do any experiments or projects, whether from this book or of your own design, under the supervision of a science teacher or other knowledgeable adult.

2. Read all instructions carefully before proceeding with a project. If you have questions, check with your supervisor before going any further.

3. Maintain a serious attitude while conducting experiments. Fooling around can be dangerous to you and to others.

4. Wear approved safety goggles when you are doing anything that might cause injury to your eyes.

5. Do not eat or drink while experimenting.

6. Have a first-aid kit nearby while you are experimenting.

7. Do not put your fingers or any object in electrical outlets.

8. Never experiment with household electricity except under

the supervision of a knowledgeable adult.

9. Do not touch a lit high-wattage bulb. Lightbulbs produce light, but they also produce heat.

10. Many substances are poisonous. Do not taste any unless instructed to do so.

1

Food, Energy, and Humans

After our human ancestors began walking on two legs, most of their waking hours were devoted to gathering food. They ate fruits, nuts, roots, seeds, and mushrooms they would gather. Occasionally, they ate the meat of small animals they hunted or trapped. Sometimes they dined on the carcass of larger animals killed by a lion, leopard, or tiger, from which they would scavenge some meat and bones. The broken animal bones found at early human sites indicate that they especially sought the marrow found inside bones. Its fatty tissue served as a rich source of energy.

We do not know when humans first controlled fire, but it was probably more than a million years ago. Light from fires kept predators away and enabled the humans to work for longer periods. Fire also changed their diet. At some point, they probably ate the meat of a wild animal that had been burned in a forest fire and discovered that cooking improved the meat's flavor. Cooking also made food softer and easier to digest, and the poisons found in some plants and seeds could be broken down by high temperatures. Parasites and bacteria in meat were killed by the heat, so the meat could be preserved for short periods. Later, they discovered that meat could be preserved for a long time by smoking and drying it. Dried meat provided nourishment during winters in Europe, when deep snow prevented hunting or food gathering.

As their technology improved, the men became predominantly hunters. The women probably stayed at a home site, caring for the young and gathering fruits, nuts, tubers, and other foods from nearby. All the food was brought to a home base. There it was shared by all members of a social group that quite likely included the children and any elderly or ill people who were unable to hunt or gather. Gathering to eat at a home site is a unique human trait that persists to this day.

The large brains that made us human and social came with a price. Brain cells require extremely large amounts of energy. Brain tissue makes up only 2 percent of our weight, but it accounts for 20 percent of the energy we need. Food in the form of leaves, roots, fruit, and berries comes in small portions. It contains relatively small amounts of energy per volume eaten. Meat, on the other hand, is a rich source of energy. To meet the energy needs of their larger brains, early humans became more carnivorous. Fortunately, their larger brains provided the intelligence they needed to become better tool makers. With tools, such as spears and knives, they were able to effectively hunt animals they could not outrun or overpower. It was their tools that allowed these early humans to increase the meat content of their diets, and thereby provide the energy their larger brains required.

1-1*
Drying Food

Our ancestors dried food to preserve it for times when food was scarce. You can see how they did this by drying a banana. To begin, peel a ripe banana and cut off the ends of the fruit. Place the peeled banana on a plastic bag, weigh it, and record the weight. Then cut the banana into slices about 0.5 cm (1/4 in) thick. Dip each piece into some lemon juice. (You will learn the reason for the lemon juice when you do Experiment 4-3.) Place the slices in a single layer on a cookie sheet.

With an adult's supervision, preheat an oven to 60°C (140°F). Place the cookie sheet in the oven and leave it there for 30 minutes. Then open the oven and turn the banana slices over with a spatula. Continue to do this at 30-minute intervals until the slices no longer stick to the metal. After that, stir the slices at 30-minute intervals.

After 8 hours, remove the cookie sheet and let the banana slices cool. Once they are cool, place them on the plastic bag you used before and weigh them. What happened to the banana's weight? Can you explain why? By what percentage did the banana's weight change?

Taste one of the dried banana slices. Describe the flavor. Early humans probably used the sun to dry food and then kept it in a cool space underground, in a deep cave, or outside in the freezing cold

Things you will need:

- an adult
- ripe banana
- balance or kitchen scale
- pen or pencil
- notebook
- knife
- lemon juice
- cookie sheet
- oven
- clock
- spatula
- plastic bags
- freezer
- refrigerator
- bread box
- twist ties

11

of winter. Place a few of the banana slices in different plastic bags and seal with twist ties. Put the slices in different places such as a freezer, refrigerator, or bread box. Which banana slices seem to remain unchanged for the longest time?

Exploring on Your Own

Repeat this experiment with a number of different foods. Which of the foods you test have the largest percentage of water? Which foods contain very little water?

Energy from Food

To provide the energy needed to make a car go, you have to put gasoline into its tank. The gasoline is then burned in the cylinders of the engine to provide the energy needed to move the pistons up and down. The motion of the pistons is transferred to the wheels and the car moves. In a somewhat similar way, you eat food that passes to your stomach and intestines, where it is digested. The digested food is carried by blood to all the cells of your body. In the cells, the digested food is "burned" to provide energy. This energy is needed so that your body can move and carry on all the chemical activities that go on inside you.

Unlike the fuel you put into a car, not all the food you eat is "burned" to produce energy. Some of it is used to build new cells— new bone, new muscle, new skin, new blood cells, new fat cells. Some kinds of food provide only energy, while others allow you to grow or replace cells that die or wear out. There are also substances (chemicals) that regulate and maintain all the many processes that go on in your body. So what you eat is as important—or more important—than how much you eat.

Food is any substance we eat that provides us with energy, the materials we need to grow new tissue or replace old tissue, or to regulate the chemical reactions and physical processes that take place in our bodies.

We obtain food from the cells that make up plant and animal tissues or from substances that these organisms produce. For example, we may eat beef, which is the muscle tissue of cows. Or we may drink milk, which is a substance secreted by cows. We can eat the flowers of zucchini plants (their petals are delicious when fried in butter and flour), or we can wait and eat the fruit (zucchini squash) that result when the eggs in the flowers are fertilized.

Some people are vegetarians. They obtain all their food from plants or plant products. Some vegetarians will eat animal products, such as milk, butter, yogurt, and honey, but not meat. Other vegetarians will eat only plants or plant products.

In the activity that follows, you will be asked to think about the source of the food that you eat.

1-2*
Where Did That Food Come From?

On a particular day, record in a vertical list in your notebook everything that you eat and drink for breakfast, lunch, dinner, and in between meals. Beside each of the items you ate, record the source of that food. Was it from an animal? Was it from a plant? (Do not forget that plants produce the grains found in bread, cakes, crackers, and other foods made with flour.) Was it something produced by an animal, such as milk, or from a plant, such as fruit? If so, what was the animal or plant that produced it?

Things you will need:
- pen or pencil
- notebook
- friends from different cultures

Did you eat any non-food substances, such as artificial coloring? If so, what were these substances? If they are not food, why do you eat them?

Keep a record of all the different kinds of food you eat during a one-week period. Ask a friend from a different culture, such as someone of Asian, African, or Middle Eastern extraction, to keep a similar record. Then compare the foods in the two lists. Are there foods in your friend's list that you do not recognize? Are there foods in your list that your friend does not recognize?

With your parents' permission, invite your friend to dinner and prepare one of the foods unfamiliar to your friend. Does he or she like the food? If you are lucky, your friend will invite you to dinner so that you can experience the taste of a food you have never eaten before.

You might also enjoy eating at restaurants that specialize in Indian, African, Chinese, Mexican, Italian, or other foreign foods. Which foods do you like? Which would you not order again?

Exploring on Your Own

Interview a number of vegetarians. Why do they not eat meat? Why do some eat animal products like cheese while others do not?

Foods

Energy is stored in the molecules of the food we eat. In our cells, these molecules react with oxygen, which is carried from our lungs to all the cells of our body by our blood. The reaction between these food molecules and oxygen is not a simple one, such as that in burning wood. It is, in fact, a series of reactions, each of which provides some energy.

There are three types of food that can provide the body with energy. They are carbohydrates, fats, and proteins. Carbohydrates and fats provide most of the energy, but only proteins contain the chemicals our bodies need to make new cells and repair old ones. The processes by which we use food to obtain energy, grow new tissue, and repair old tissue depend on certain other essential nutrients known as vitamins and minerals.

Of course, we also need water, which makes up well over half the weight of our bodies. More than two thirds of the food we eat is actually water. The water we ingest comes from three sources: the liquids we drink, foods that contain water, and water produced in the body by chemical reactions that take place there. For example, when we "burn" sugar to obtain energy, water is produced as a by-product.

Carbohydrates: A Source of Energy

Carbohydrates are the most abundant and economical of the three foods. Carbohydrates are compounds; that is, they are made of elements that have combined chemically in a particular ratio. The *carbo-* part of the term *carbohydrate* tells you that these compounds contain carbon. The *-hydrate* part indicates the presence of water. Since water contains hydrogen and oxygen, carbohydrates consist of the elements carbon (C), hydrogen (H), and oxygen (O). (The letters in parentheses are the chemical symbols for the elements named.) In carbohydrates, there are two hydrogen atoms for every oxygen atom, just as there are in water (H_2O).

15

Carbohydrates are either simple sugars, such as glucose, dextrose, fructose, or levulose, or substances that will react with water to form simple sugars. The simple sugars are called monosaccharides (see Figure 1a). The monosaccharides found in foods such as fruits have 6 carbon atoms, 12 hydrogen atoms, and 6 oxygen atoms ($C_6H_{12}O_6$). All these simple sugars have these same numbers of atoms of carbon, hydrogen, and oxygen. The compounds are different, however, because their atoms are arranged differently.

Disaccharide molecules (Figure 1b) form when two monosaccharide molecules combine and lose a molecule of water. The molecules of sucrose—ordinary table sugar—form a disaccharide.

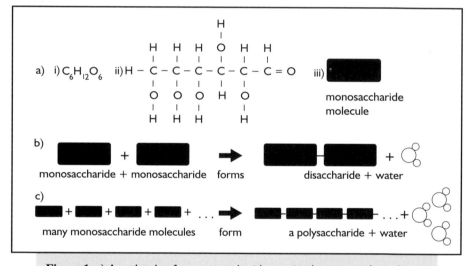

Figure 1. a) A molecule of a monosaccharide, or simple sugar, such as glucose contains 6 carbon atoms, 12 hydrogen atoms, and 6 oxygen atoms. The molecule can be represented in several different ways: i) The molecular formula for a monosaccharide; ii) A structural formula showing how the atoms in glucose, a particular sugar, are arranged; iii) A rectangle can be used to represent any monosaccharide molecule. b) Two monosaccharide molecules combine to form a disaccharide molecule and a molecule of water. c) Many monosaccharide molecules combine to form a polysaccharide molecule, such as starch, while producing a molecule of water for each monosaccharide molecule formed.

Sucrose has 12 carbon atoms, 22 hydrogen atoms, and 11 oxygen atoms ($C_{12}H_{22}O_{11}$). Lactose, the sugar found in milk, and maltose, the sugar found in malts and germinating cereals, are also disaccharides. Disaccharides must be changed (digested) to monosaccharides in your body before their energy can be tapped.

Polysaccharides (Figure 1c) are molecules made of many units of monosaccharide sugars joined together. Each monosaccharide molecule loses a molecule of water when it joins to another monosaccharide molecule to form a polysaccharide molecule. The most common polysaccharide in food is starch, which is stored in plant cells, and cellulose, which makes up the cell walls in plants. When our bodies digest starch, the starch is changed to simple sugars; that is, the polysaccharide molecules are converted to monosaccharide molecules. Humans are unable to digest cellulose. However, cellulose provides fiber, which helps to move food along the intestines. Unlike plants, we store carbohydrates as glycogen, another polysaccharide that is found in our livers and muscles.

1-3*
Where Do Carbohydrates Come From?

Our bodies are not able to make sugars and starches (carbohydrates). Only plants with the green pigment chlorophyll can manufacture carbohydrates. Most of the carbohydrates we eat come from plants. If you look at the list of the food you ate from Experiment 1-2, you will find that the foods came either from plants, or from animals that ate plants or plant products such as grain.

The leaves of plants are food factories. Cells in the leaves are able to take carbon dioxide gas from the air and combine it with water in the presence of light to make sugar, which is stored in plant cells as starch. The carbon dioxide provides the carbon and oxygen found in carbohydrates, and the water provides the hydrogen. During this process, which is called photosynthesis, the plants release oxygen into the atmosphere. The oxygen also comes from the water.

Leaves are green because they contain pigments that absorb most of the colors in white light except green. Because green light is reflected instead of being absorbed, most leaves appear green. The green pigment in plant cells that is essential to photosynthesis is chlorophyll. Chlorophyll absorbs light, which is converted to the energy stored in molecules of starch during photosynthesis.

Any excess sugar produced in a leaf is changed to starch and stored. You can use a common test for starch to confirm that food

Things you will need:

- results of Experiment 1-2
- paper clip
- black construction paper or aluminum foil
- geranium plant
- an adult
- gloves or oven mitt
- safety glasses
- tongs
- stove
- pan
- water
- rubbing alcohol
- small jar
- tincture of iodine

18

is produced in leaves when light, carbon dioxide, and water are present. Use a paper clip to hold a small folded piece of black construction paper or aluminum foil over both sides of a geranium leaf still on the plant, as shown in Figure 2. Be careful not to damage the leaf when you attach the paper or foil. Do this in the morning on a bright sunny day when lots of light will fall on the leaves.

After four or five hours, pick the leaf from the plant, bring it indoors, and remove the foil or paper. Put on gloves or an oven mitt and safety glasses. Then, **under adult supervision**, use tongs to hold the leaf's stem so that you can immerse the rest of the leaf into a pan of boiling water on a stove. Hold the leaf under the boiling water for about a minute. The heat will break open cell walls within the leaf.

Now that the cell walls are broken, you can remove the green chlorophyll from the leaf. But first **turn off the stove**. The rubbing

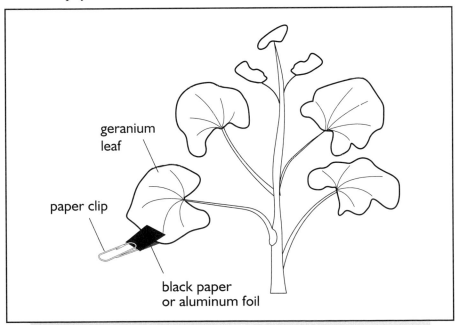

Figure 2. Use black paper or aluminum foil to prevent light from reaching part of a geranium leaf.

alcohol you will use to extract the pigment is flammable. It should **never** be brought near a flame or red-hot burner.

Prepare a small jar of alcohol, place the limp leaf in it, and leave it overnight. The next morning you will find the alcohol has a green color due to the pigments it has extracted from the leaf.

In a saucer, mix together approximately equal amounts of tincture of iodine and water; about 5 milliliters (mL) of each will do. **Remember: Iodine is poisonous. Handle it carefully!** Next, rinse the leaf in warm water to remove the alcohol. Then spread it out and place it in the iodine-water solution.

If the leaf contained starch, you will see it turn a dark blue-black color—the color that forms when iodine reacts with starch. Was there starch in the leaf cells? Is one area of the leaf much lighter than the rest? Can you identify that region? In which area of the leaf did photosynthesis not take place? What evidence do you have to show that light is required for photosynthesis?

Exploring on Your Own

How do we know that the oxygen released during photosynthesis comes from the water in the plant and not from the carbon dioxide, or from both water and carbon dioxide?

Design an experiment to show that plants need carbon dioxide in order to perform photosynthesis. Then, **under adult supervision**, carry out your experiment.

Design an experiment to show that chlorophyll is needed for plants to perform photosynthesis. Then, **under adult supervision**, carry out your experiment.

1-4
Testing for Carbohydrates

Testing for Starch

From the previous experiment, you know that iodine can be used to test for starch. Prepare a dilute iodine solution by mixing about 10 drops of tincture of iodine with 100 drops of water. **Be careful handling iodine. It is a poison.**

You can use this iodine solution to test for starch in foods. In separate saucers, crush or pour samples of potato, bread, milk, cooked white meat such as chicken breast, and a piece of an unsalted cracker. Into still another container, spit out a piece of another unsalted cracker that you have chewed for about five minutes.

Mix each of these food samples with a little water. Then test each sample with a drop of the iodine solution. **Remember not to put anything with iodine on it into your mouth!**

Which foods contain starch? What other foods might you try?

Testing for Sugar

If you can obtain Clinistix from a drug store, you can use them to test for simple sugars. Just dip the stick in a sample of liquid that

Things you will need:

- medicine cups or small containers
- eyedropper
- tincture of iodine
- water
- teaspoon
- cornstarch
- potato
- bread
- milk
- cooked white meat of chicken
- unsalted crackers
- Clinistix (from a drug store); or Benedict's solution (from school)
- an adult
- stove
- small cooking pan
- corn syrup or maple syrup
- test tube or small glass
- sucrose (table sugar)
- saucers
- toothpicks

you think may contain simple sugars. If Clinistix are not available, your school may have Benedict's solution. **With your teacher's permission and supervision**, you can use Benedict's solution to test for simple sugars. Pour about 5 mL of corn syrup or maple syrup into a test tube or a small glass. Add about 5 mL of the Benedict's solution and place the tube or glass in a small pan that holds some water. Place the pan on a stove and heat the water to boiling. If a simple (monosaccharide) sugar is present, the liquid will turn green, yellow, red, or orange. An orange color indicates a high concentration of simple sugar.

Repeat the experiment using 5 mL of a saturated solution of sucrose (table sugar). Does this sugar solution contain any simple sugars?

In separate dishes, crush samples of potato, bread, milk, and cooked white chicken meat. Into another dish spit out an unsalted cracker that you have chewed for about five minutes. Mix each of these samples with a little water and test with Clinistix or Benedict's solution as you did previously.

Mix 1/4 teaspoonful of cornstarch with an equal amount of corn syrup or maple syrup, each of which, as you know from an earlier test, contains a simple sugar. Add some water and stir the mixture with a toothpick. Pour a small amount of the mixture onto a saucer and add a drop of iodine solution. **Remember: Iodine is poisonous!** Do you get a positive test for starch when it is mixed with sugar? Test for a simple sugar with Clinistix or, **under your teacher's supervision**, test using Benedict's solution. Do you get a positive test for a simple sugar when it is mixed with starch?

1-5
Heating Carbohydrates

Many compounds can be broken down (decomposed) into simpler substances by heating them. From what you know about their composition, what do you predict will happen if you decompose a carbohydrate by heating it?

To test your prediction, make a number of small pans with handles by folding pieces of heavy-duty aluminum foil, as shown in Figure 3a. Use a clothespin to grasp the pan's handle. This will allow you to safely hold the pan over a flame. Place a very small amount of ordinary sugar (sucrose) in one of the pans. Place a candle in a candle holder. Put **safety glasses** over your eyes and an **oven mitt** on your hand. Then, **under adult supervision**, light the candle and heat the sugar by holding the pan above the candle flame, as shown in Figure 3b.

What happens to the sugar when you heat it? Is there any evidence of vapor coming from the decomposing sugar? If there is, ask a friend to hold a cooking pan of cold water over the vapor. Does

Things you will need:

- heavy-duty aluminum foil
- clothespin
- table sugar (sucrose)
- candle and candle holder
- safety glasses
- oven mitt
- an adult
- matches
- a friend
- metal cooking pan
- cold water
- cobalt chloride paper strips (your school may let you have a few)
- cornstarch
- flour
- bread
- raw potato
- corn syrup
- unflavored gelatin powder
- watercolor brush
- lemon juice
- white paper
- tongs
- incandescent lightbulb

23

any liquid condense on the bottom of the pan? If it does, what do you think that liquid might be?

If strips of blue cobalt chloride paper are available, place the end of a strip in the liquid. Cobalt chloride paper turns pink in water. Can you identify the liquid now? What confirming tests might you do?

Did the sugar change? Does it eventually turn black? What do you think the black substance is?

Repeat the experiment, this time with a very small amount of cornstarch in place of the sugar. What happens to the cornstarch when you heat it?

Try heating very small amounts of other carbohydrates and carbohydrate-rich foods such as flour, bread, raw potato, and a drop of corn syrup. What seems to be the common substance that remains

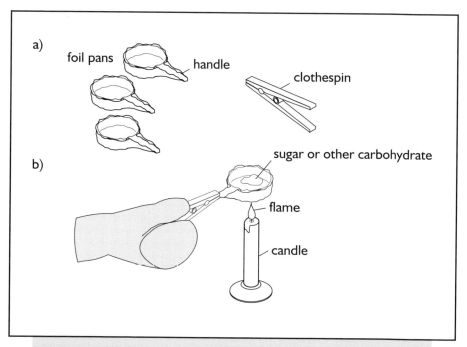

Figure 3. a) Make small pans by folding a piece of heavy-duty aluminum foil. b) Use a clothespin to hold a pan with a sample of sugar over a flame.

after all these carbohydrates are heated? What else do you think is produced when these carbohydrates decompose?

Do other foods behave in the same way? To find out, you might try heating a protein such as gelatin powder. Does the gelatin powder decompose in a way similar to carbohydrate decomposition?

Heating a food to decompose it is the secret of many invisible inks. Dissolve a teaspoonful of sugar in two ounces of hot water. Using a watercolor paintbrush as a pen and the sugar solution as ink, write a short message on a piece of white paper. After the "ink" has dried, heat the paper **under adult supervision** by holding it with tongs above a candle flame. Why does the message slowly appear?

Measuring Energy: The Calorie

There are many forms of energy—light, gravitational, kinetic, electrical, elastic, and so on. All these different forms of energy can be converted to heat (thermal energy). Consequently, heat is a useful way to measure energy. You can measure heat in units known as calories. A calorie is the quantity of heat required to raise the temperature of one gram (g) of water by one degree Celsius (°C). If you add heat to water, the water's temperature will rise. If you remove heat from water, its temperature will fall. If the temperature of 1 g of water rises 1°C, 1 calorie of heat has been added to the water. If the temperature of 10 g of water rises 10°C, 100 calories of heat have been added. The product of the mass of the water and its temperature change can be used to measure heat.

Heat (in calories) = **mass of water** (in grams) x **temperature change** (in °C).

Nutritionists, dietitians, doctors, and other people who work with food need to know how much energy is stored in the foods people eat. They measure energy in Calories. Notice that the unit of energy they use is spelled with a capital C. It is sometimes called a *large calorie*, or a *kilocalorie*. It is equal to 1,000 calories. It can be defined as the heat required to raise the temperature of 1.0 kilogram (1,000 g) of water through 1°C. A dietitian may say that a tablespoon of peanut butter contains 90 Calories. He or she means that if the energy stored in that peanut butter is converted to heat, the heat generated would be enough to raise the temperature of 10 kg of water 9°C.

We say food is "burned" in our bodies; however, there are no flames. The food does combine with oxygen to produce carbon dioxide and water eventually. But it does so in a series of reactions. Each reaction releases a small amount of energy that keeps our bodies warm or allows our muscles to contract, our brains to think, and our cells to carry on the many processes that take place there. In the end, the total energy the food provides is equal to the heat it releases when it burns outside the body.

To find the energy available in a food, the food is weighed and placed in a metal container known as a bomb calorimeter (Figure 4). Oxygen is added to the calorimeter, which is surrounded by water. The outer wall of the calorimeter is well insulated so that very little heat can escape. The food is ignited and burns in the calorimeter. The heat released is absorbed by the water surrounding the reaction. The change in the water's temperature when multiplied by the mass of the water will allow the experimenter to determine the energy released when the food burns.

Suppose that 1.5 g of food burns. Its heat is absorbed by 1.0 kg of water, which undergoes a temperature change of 6.15°C. The heat released by the food is:

$$1.0 \text{ kg} \times 6.15°C = 6.15 \text{ Cal.}$$

The heat released in terms of Calories per gram of food is:

$$6.15 \text{ Cal} \div 1.5 \text{ g} = 4.1 \text{ Cal/g.}$$

The experimenter knows that the food that burned is a carbohydrate because carbohydrates typically release 4.1 Cal/g. A

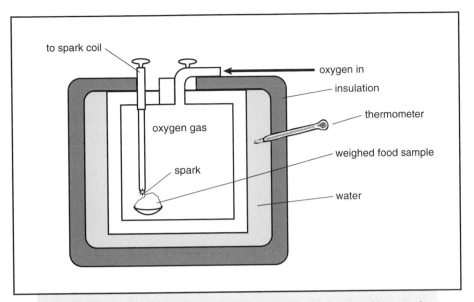

Figure 4. In a bomb calorimeter, a weighed sample of food is ignited by a spark. The food burns in oxygen and the heat released warms a known amount of water that surrounds the chamber where the food burns. By knowing the temperature change of the water, the heat released by the food can be calculated.

fat would have released 9.45 Cal/g, and a protein would have released 5.65 Cal/g. Protein, however, is never completely "burned" in the body. Some always remains in the form of urea, uric acid, or creatinine. These waste products, which still contain about 1.3 Cal/g, are excreted in the urine. As a result, our bodies can only obtain about 4.3 Cal/g from protein. Generally, nutritionists round off energy values and say that carbohydrates and proteins release about 4 Cal/g and fats provide 9 Cal/g.

1-6*
The Energy Stored in a Corn Puff

In your body, food is digested, absorbed into your blood, and carried to cells where it is oxidized slowly in a series of chemical reactions that release the energy stored in the molecules of food. You can find the energy stored in a piece of food by burning it in air or oxygen and measuring the energy released.

To find the energy stored in a corn puff, you can build a simple calorimeter like the one shown in Figure 5. A small, empty 6-oz frozen juice can with a metal bottom and cardboard sides can be used to hold cold water. **Ask an adult** to use a nail to punch holes through opposite sides of the can near its open top. Push a pencil through the holes. The pencil will support this small can inside a large (#10) can.

Ask an adult to remove both ends of the large can. Use a can opener to make four or five triangular holes along the sides of the large can near its bottom end,

Things you will need:

- small (6-oz) frozen juice can with a metal bottom and cardboard sides
- large nail
- pencil
- large (#10) tin can
- can opener
- a cork
- aluminum foil
- pliers
- large sewing needle
- balance or scale
- cold water
- graduated cylinder or measuring cup
- laboratory thermometer ($^-$10–110°C)
- an adult
- matches
- corn puffs
- pencil or pen
- notebook
- peanuts
- walnuts
- cashews

as shown in Figure 5. The holes will allow air to enter the can so the corn puff will burn. The bright interior of the large can will reflect heat that might otherwise escape to the surrounding air.

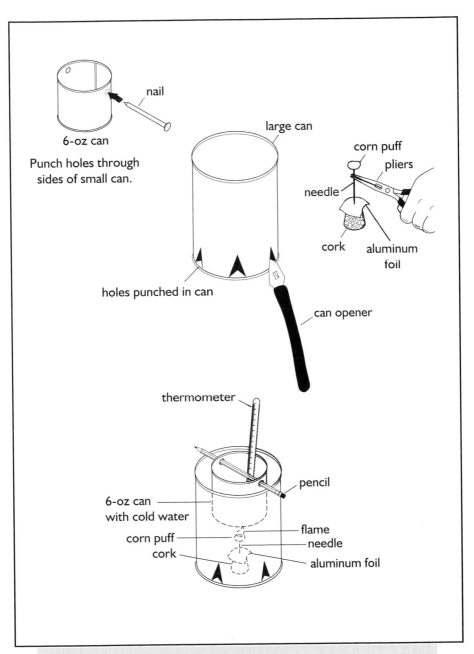

Figure 5. The energy stored in food can be measured by burning the food and capturing the heat released in a known amount of water.

To support the corn puff, cover the small end of a cork with a piece of aluminum foil. With pliers, force the eye of a large sewing needle through the foil and into the cork, as shown. Next, break the corn puff in half. Weigh one of the halves on a sensitive balance. If the balance is not sensitive enough to weigh one corn puff, weigh a hundred of them and divide by 200 to find the weight of half of one. Next, push the corn puff half down gently onto the sharp upright end of the needle. Pour 150 g of cold water into the small can. Since 1.0 mL of water weighs 1 g, you can simply measure out a volume of 150 mL (3.5 oz) of cold water and pour it into the can. Place a laboratory thermometer in the can and measure the water's temperature.

Ask an adult to light the corn puff with a match. Immediately place the large can over the burning corn puff and put the small can with the water into the large can, as shown in Figure 5. Stir the water gently with the thermometer until after the corn puff goes out. Does any of the corn puff remain? If it does, can you identify what the remaining mass is?

Record the final temperature of the water. The mass of water and its temperature change can be used to calculate the heat released by the burning corn puff. Remember, a calorie is the amount of heat required to raise the temperature of 1 g of water by 1°C. If the temperature of the 150 g of water increased by 10°C, then the corn puff provided 1,500 calories (150 g x 10°C) of energy. How much heat did the burning corn puff release?

If any of the corn puff remains, reweigh it. What mass of corn puff, in grams, provided the heat absorbed by the water? How much heat was produced per gram of corn puff burned? Do you think the value of the heat per gram that you obtained from your data is higher or lower than the actual value? What makes you think so?

Nutritionists measure energy in what are called large calories or Calories. A Calorie with a capital "C" is the heat needed to raise the temperature of 1 *kilogram* of water by 1°C, so it is 1,000 times bigger than a calorie with a small "c." How many Calories are provided by 1 gram of corn puff according to your data?

Under adult supervision, find the heat released per gram, in calories per gram, by a peanut. Try a walnut, then a cashew. How do they each compare with energy per gram produced by a corn puff?

Exploring on Your Own

With an adult present, use the equipment you used in Experiment 1-6 to measure the amount of heat, in calories, released *per gram* of candle wax for several different kinds of candles.

If we can obtain energy from candle wax, why don't we use it as a food?

2

Fats, Proteins, Vitamins, and Minerals

Carbohydrates make up the bulk of the food we consume and provide most of the energy our bodies need. However, we cannot live for long on a diet of only carbohydrates. We need protein to provide the matter needed for growth and the repair of cells. Enzymes that help digest food and regulate other chemical processes that take place within our bodies are also proteins. And we need at least small amounts of fat to make adipose tissue, the soft tissue that insulates our bodies and cushions our internal organs. Fat is also required to carry certain fat-soluble vitamins to our cells. Both fat-soluble and water-soluble vitamins are needed to regulate the many chemical reactions that go on within our bodies and make life possible. We also require a great variety of minerals, including calcium, iron, magnesium, and potassium. Macrominerals such as calcium, phosphorus, salt (sodium chloride), potassium, and magnesium are needed in relatively large amounts. For example, we require more than a gram of calcium and phosphorus each day to build and maintain our bones and teeth. Trace minerals, such as iron, iodine, and zinc, are essential to life, but only a few milligrams or less of these are needed in our daily diet. About 10 to 20 mg of iron is sufficient to combine with proteins to make the hemoglobin found in the red blood cells we produce continually in our bone marrow. And less than a milligram of iodine, readily provided by iodized salt, is needed to keep our thyroid glands functioning properly.

In this chapter, you will learn more about these various food substances. You will carry out experiments to test for the presence of fats and proteins, and you will use a chemical test to find out which juices have the largest concentration of vitamin C.

Fats: Another Source of Energy and a Means of Storing It

Fats are compounds that contain carbon, hydrogen, and oxygen, but not in the same ratio as carbohydrates. If you have ever eaten over-cooked bacon, you are aware that fat contains carbon, which is the black substance that remains after fat has been decomposed by heating. Fats contain more carbon and hydrogen but less oxygen per gram than carbohydrates. As a result, they provide more energy than carbohydrates or proteins.

If you eat more food than your body needs, the excess is stored as fat in cells that make up what is called adipose tissue. Everyone has some adipose tissue beneath the skin, as well as on and in internal organs such as the kidneys and intestines. The fat serves to protect and cushion these organs and acts as a way of storing energy.

2-1*
Testing for Fatty Food

Chemists have ways of testing for fats, but they involve substances that are explosive or toxic. There is, however, one simple test that can be used to identify many fatty foods. Tear off one side of a brown paper bag. Put a drop of cooking oil on your finger and rub it in circular fashion on one small section of the brown paper. Use another finger to rub some water into another part of the paper in the same way. If you hold the paper up to the light, you will see that the spot made with the cooking oil and, perhaps, the one made with water as well, are translucent—they transmit light. The liquids transmit light because they fill in the spaces between the wood fibers in the paper that trap the light. The water spot will become opaque as the liquid evaporates, but the oily spot, which contains fat, will remain

Things you will need:
- brown paper bag
- cooking oil
- water
- bacon
- hot dog
- peanut butter
- butter
- margarine
- lard
- milk
- cream
- orange juice
- lemonade
- mayonnaise
- low-fat mayonnaise
- egg whites
- egg yolks
- lamp with a 100-watt bulb
- lamp with a 40-watt or a 60-watt bulb
- long table
- dark room
- ruler

translucent. Why do you think the oily spot remains translucent?

Try testing some other substances. Make circles in the brown paper using uncooked bacon and a cross-section of an uncooked hot dog. Try some peanut butter, ordinary butter, margarine, and lard.

Also try milk, a walnut, cream, orange juice, lemonade, mayonnaise, low-fat mayonnaise, egg whites, and egg yolks. Which of these substances give a positive test for fat? Which appear to have little or no fat?

Exploring on Your Own

A photometer is a device that can be used to compare the brightness of two light sources, such as two lightbulbs. How can you use an oily spot on a piece of brown paper as a simple photometer?

Use your photometer to find the intensity of light from a full moon, which is approximately 380,000 km from Earth, as compared to the light from a 60-watt bulb.

Proteins: Food for Energy and for Making New Tissue

In addition to carbon, hydrogen, and oxygen, proteins always contain nitrogen and sometimes sulfur, phosphorus, or iron. Protein molecules consist of chains of amino acid molecules joined together, as shown in Figure 6. These molecules are very large. A molecule of albumin, the protein found in egg white, weighs about as much as 2,400 water molecules. Hemoglobin molecules, one of the proteins found in red blood cells, weigh about 3,500 times as much as water molecules.

The proteins found in the human body are formed from 20 different amino acids. About half of those amino acids must be obtained from the food we eat. The others can be made from other substances in our diet. Rich sources of protein are milk, meat, fish, eggs, cereal, and in some vegetables such as legumes (peas, beans, lentils, and peanuts).

Protein-rich foods, such as meat, fish, milk, cheese, yogurt, and eggs, are difficult and expensive to produce. That is one cause of malnutrition among people in poor countries. They cannot afford the protein they need to build, replace, or repair bone, muscle, and connective tissue.

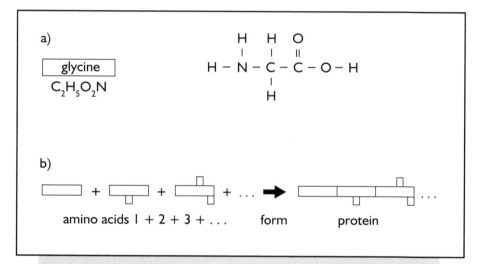

Figure 6. a) The structural and molecular formulas of glycine, one of the simplest amino acids, are shown. We can also represent an amino acid with a rectangle. b) Many amino acid molecules join together to form a protein molecule.

2-2

Testing for Proteins

The Biuret test can be used to identify protein in food. Because the test involves the use of sodium hydroxide (lye) solution, which is harmful to skin and eyes, you will need **an adult to help you** with this experiment. Both you and the adult should wear safety glasses and rubber gloves throughout the experiment. The adult should prepare the sodium hydroxide (NaOH) solution by adding 10 g of the white solid to 100 g of cold water and stirring until the solid is dissolved.

While the adult is preparing the sodium hydroxide solution, you can prepare a 3-percent solution of copper sulfate by adding 3 g of blue copper sulfate ($CuSO_4 \cdot 5H_2O$) crystals to 100 mL of water.

Egg white from a raw egg is a good source of protein. It can be used to reveal what a positive test for protein looks like. Separate the white of an egg from its yolk. To do this, use a butter knife to crack an egg at its center. Hold the egg upright over a

Things you will need:

- an adult
- safety glasses
- balance
- rubber gloves
- sodium hydroxide (NaOH) crystals (obtain from school science laboratory)
- copper sulfate crystals ($CuSO_4 \cdot 5H_2O$) (obtain from school science laboratory)
- cold water
- an egg
- butterknife
- bowl
- soap
- 2 glass jars
- metric measuring cup or graduated cylinder
- large test tube or small jar or bottle
- stopper
- eyedropper
- flour
- gelatin
- potato
- bread
- milk
- cooked white meat of chicken
- crackers
- sugar

37

bowl. Remove the upper half of the shell. Some egg white will fall into the bowl when you remove the upper half of the shell. Now carefully pour the yolk, trying not to break it, from one half of the shell to the other several times over the bowl. As you do so, more egg white will fall into the bowl. When most of the white has been removed, discard the yolk, which is primarily fat, or save it for cooking. **Always wash your hands after handling raw eggs.**

Pour the egg white into a large test tube or a small jar or bottle. Add an equal volume of water, stopper the tube and shake it to thoroughly mix egg white and water. **Have the adult** add an equal volume of the sodium hydroxide solution; stopper, and shake the tube again. Then add about 5 drops of the copper sulfate solution; stopper, and shake once more. A violet or blue-violet color indicates the presence of protein. The darker the color, the greater the concentration of protein.

Mash samples of different foods separately in water. You might use flour, gelatin, pieces of potato, bread, milk, cooked white meat of chicken, crackers, and sugar. **Ask the adult** to help you test these foods for protein. Which foods give a positive test for protein? Which foods can you conclude do not contain protein?

2-3*
Proteins and the Tyndall Effect

John Tyndall was a nineteenth-century British physicist who discovered that if a beam of light passes through water or any clear liquid containing small molecules, the beam cannot be seen from the side of the clear vessel holding the liquid. Larger particles, however, do reflect some of the light, making the beam visible—just as a beam of sunlight can be seen when it shines through dust particles in a room.

To observe what Tyndall saw, pour a teaspoonful of sugar into a small glass or beaker. Fill the vessel about halfway with warm water and stir the mixture with a spoon. As you can see, the sugar dissolves in the water to form a clear solution.

Things you will need:

• teaspoon

• sugar

• small glass or beaker

• warm water

• bowl

• knife

• spoon

• egg

• cup

• eyedropper

• small test tube

• glass of water

• dark area

• penlight or small flashlight

Next, separate the white of an egg from the yolk, as described in Experiment 2-2. Use an eyedropper to transfer the egg white to a small test tube.

Take both liquids and a glass of water to a dark area. Use a penlight or a small flashlight to shine a narrow beam of light through the sugar solution while you view the liquid from the side, as shown in Figure 7. If you can see the beam in the liquid when you view it from the side, you are observing what is known as the Tyndall effect.

Is there a Tyndall effect when you shine the light through the sugar solution? Is there a Tyndall effect when you shine the light through a glass of water?

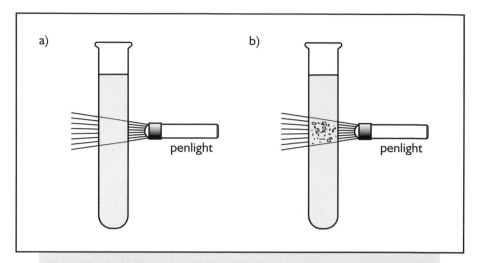

Figure 7. a) A beam of light passing through water or a clear solution cannot be seen from the side. The particles in the liquid are too small to reflect any light. b) Large particles do reflect some light, making the beam visible from the side.

Remembering that protein molecules, such as those found in egg white, are some of the largest molecules known, would you expect to observe the Tyndall effect when you shine the light through the egg white? Try it. Was your prediction correct?

Exploring On Your Own

How did John Tyndall use his discovery to explain atmospheric phenomena, such as the fact that the sky appears to be blue?

What other contributions did Tyndall make to science?

Minerals

There are 92 natural elements, but 96 percent of your body is composed of only four elements—oxygen, carbon, hydrogen, and nitrogen. The remaining 4 percent contain trace amounts of 60 different elements. The use of some of these elements in the body is known. Others are probably essential for health, but their functions remain unknown.

The elements that are essential to a good diet, other than those in carbohydrates, fats, and proteins, provide no energy, but are required for other reasons. They may be needed to maintain or build strong bones and teeth, or to help regulate the many chemical processes that take place in our cells and body fluids.

Calcium (Ca), the major mineral found in bones and teeth, is also needed for a variety of activities that go on in our cells. People who are growing require at least 1.2 g (1200 mg) of calcium per day because they are making new bone and tooth tissue. It is for this reason that young people are advised to drink lots of milk. Milk is the best source of calcium, but dark green leafy vegetables, shellfish, citrus fruits, and legumes also contain calcium.

Phosphorus (P), too, is essential for the growth of bones and teeth as well as for regulating chemical processes. A growing person's daily diet should contain at least one gram of phosphorus. Phosphorus is present in milk, dairy products, meat, fish, poultry, egg yolks, and whole-grain breads and cereals.

Iron (Fe) is an element found in hemoglobin, the protein in red blood cells. It is hemoglobin that combines with oxygen in the lungs and transports this vital element to all the cells of the body. Foods that contain iron include whole grains, egg yolk, beef (especially beef liver), shellfish, fruits, and green vegetables.

Iodine (I) is found in thyroxin, a hormone secreted by the thyroid gland that regulates the body's use of food. We need only about 0.000014 gram of iodine per day to meet the needs of the thyroid gland. Consequently, most water supplies contain all the iodine required in the daily diet. In regions where iodine is in short supply, the thyroid may enlarge, producing a swelling in the neck known as a goiter. The condition can be avoided by eating a diet that contains fish, or by using iodized salt.

Copper (Cu) is required for the manufacture of hemoglobin even though it is not an ingredient of the protein. This element is present in compounds found in liver, nuts, legumes, fruits, and dark green leafy vegetables.

Zinc (Zn), which is found in whole grains, peas, fish, and lean meats, is needed for growth, tissue healing, and proper development of red blood cells.

To provide fluorine (F), which prevents tooth decay, many communities add fluoride salts to their water supply. The decline in tooth decay among children can be attributed to this practice and, some dentists believe, to the widespread use of fluoride treatments.

Sodium (Na), potassium (K), magnesium (Mg), chlorine (Cl), and trace quantities of a few more elements are also essential. They are involved in the processes that take place in and between muscle, nerve, blood, and other cells. These elements generally enter the body combined with other elements in compounds. For example, sodium and chlorine enter the body as ordinary salt, a compound chemically known as sodium chloride (NaCl).

Vitamins

In 1912, Casimir Funk, a Polish chemist, suggested that many unexplained diseases such as beriberi, scurvy, and rickets were caused by a lack of certain unknown substances in the diet. He referred to these substances as *vitamines* because he thought they were amines (a type of chemical) essential to life. Later, the word was shortened to vitamins.

Vitamin B_1 was the first vitamin to be discovered. In 1896, Christiaan Eijkman, a Dutch physician, was in the East Indies trying to determine what germ caused beriberi. Beriberi is a disease that affects the nerves leading to and from the arms and legs. It causes loss of sensation and paralysis that is often followed by heart failure. Eijkman was unable to find any germ associated with beriberi. However, during his research there was a sudden outbreak of beriberi in the chickens he was using in his experiments. He found that these birds, who were being fed polished rice, were cured quickly when they ate unpolished (whole grain) rice.

A decade later, an English biochemist, Frederick Hopkins, recognized that the disorder was a dietary deficiency. Something in the hull of the rice provided the necessary trace amount of what Funk later referred to as a vitamin. In 1926 the trace substance needed to prevent beriberi was isolated. It turned out to be a complex substance known as thiamine, which is found in such foods as whole grains (including rice), milk, liver, pork, and pasta. Since our daily requirement of thiamine is only 1.5 mg, deficiency of the vitamin is very rare.

Most vitamins cannot be made (synthesized) by the human body, but there are exceptions. Vitamin D can be produced in the body if sunlight reaches substances in the skin that can be made into vitamin D (calciferol). Vitamins B12 and K are synthesized by bacteria normally present in the intestine. But most vitamins are found in food. They are needed for growth and normal body activities.

Enzymes in the body catalyze (speed up) certain chemical reactions, like the digestion of food. Vitamins are cofactors that help the enzymes work. Without cofactors, which also serve as catalysts, the reactions would go much too slowly.

Vitamins A, D, E, and K are fat-soluble. This means that they dissolve in fats and will collect in fat cells in the body. These vitamins can be harmful if taken in excess of body needs because they will accumulate in adipose (fat) tissue. Vitamins A and D are usually added to enrich low-fat milk because they are removed from whole milk along with the fat. The other vitamins are water-soluble. If large amounts of these vitamins are ingested, the excess will dissolve, be carried away by body fluids, and be excreted in the urine.

Vitamin B_2, riboflavin, is found in meat, especially liver, milk, eggs, dark green leafy vegetables, and whole grains. It is needed for the proper use of food and oxygen by the body. Lack of riboflavin causes severe skin problems, poor growth in children, nerve degeneration, and sensitivity to light. Since 1.7 mg of riboflavin meets our daily needs, few people suffer from lack of this vitamin.

Vitamin B_3, niacin, is present in whole grains, liver, fish, nuts, eggs, and legumes. It is essential in preventing pellagra, a disease that causes skin disorders, excessive salivation, diarrhea, vomiting, and mental confusion including hallucinations. A normal diet that provides 20 mg or more of niacin is readily provided by the foods mentioned above. As a result, pellagra has been virtually eliminated from most industrial nations.

Pyridoxine (vitamin B_6), cobalamin (vitamin B_{12}), and folacin (folic acid), along with the other B vitamins, are all part of the vitamin B complex. Pyridoxine, found in whole grains, meats, spinach, green beans, and bananas, is necessary for the proper utilization of food by the body. Symptoms of its deficiency include nervousness, irritability, skin lesions, and, in children, convulsions.

Vitamin B_{12}, present in meat, fish, and milk products, is required for the manufacture of proteins and red blood cells. A deficiency can result in anemia (a low number of red blood cells), weakness, and intestinal disorders.

Folic acid (folacin) is required for the manufacture of nucleic acid, the utilization of protein, and the manufacture of red blood cells. It is present in liver, milk, eggs, fish, legumes, wheat germ, and cheese, but it can be destroyed by extensive cooking. Symptoms of its deficiency include anemia, weakness, and diarrhea. Recent studies by epidemiologist David Snowdon at the University of Kentucky suggest that Alzheimer's disease, which affects the brains of many elderly people, is related to low levels of folic acid.

His studies also indicate that subjects (nuns from the School Sisters of Notre Dame) with the highest level of folic acid were the least likely to exhibit the mental declines associated with Alzheimer's.

Other research indicates that high levels of folic acid are effective in reducing the likelihood of breast and colon cancer. Furthermore, evidence of a link between a lack of folic acid and neural tube defects in fetuses are so strong that the Food and Drug Administration now requires that many grain products be fortified with folic acid.

Vitamin C, ascorbic acid, is found in citrus fruits, tomatoes, green peppers, melons, and strawberries. We need at least 60 mg of this vitamin each day. Lack of vitamin C causes scurvy, a disease characterized by bleeding gums, loose teeth, and hemorrhaging into joints and muscles. These symptoms arise because ascorbic acid is required for the formation and maintenance of collagen, the connective tissue that holds cells together.

Early records of long sea voyages reveal that there were often epidemics of scurvy aboard ships. British sailors came to be known as "limeys" because a physician in their navy discovered that scurvy could be prevented by including lemons and limes in their diet.

Nobel chemist Linus Pauling claimed that large doses of vitamin C could prevent the common cold. However, a number of medical researchers have not been able to find evidence to support Pauling's claim. In fact, there is evidence that an excess of ascorbic acid can cause kidney stones and anemia due to the breakdown of red blood cells.

Vitamin A, retinol, is found in large amounts in fish-liver oils. However, any diet that includes vegetables and dairy products will provide adequate quantities of vitamin A or a precursor of the vitamin. Carotene, an orange pigment present in vegetables such as carrots, can be changed into vitamin A in the body. The vitamin is needed for bone and tooth development, maintenance of skin and membranes, and to prevent night blindness. Rod cells in the periphery of the eye contain visual purple, a substance that breaks down in the presence of light. Without vitamin A, visual purple cannot be synthesized. The result is an inability to convert light to the nervous impulses that allow us to see in dim light.

Vitamin D, calciferol, is needed to maintain the proper concentration of calcium and phosphorus in the blood and in bones and teeth. Lack of the vitamin can cause rickets, a disease associated with soft bones, that causes legs to bow and deformities to appear in the rib cage and skull. Vitamin D can be made in the body if individuals receive sufficient sunlight. It is also found in fish-liver oils, fortified milk, liver, and egg yolks.

Vitamin E, tocopherol, which is found in seed and vegetable oils and many other foods, is believed to be essential in maintaining the strength of cell walls, and has been advocated for a variety of body disorders.

Vitamin K, a complex organic chemical (methyl-phytyl-naphthoquinone), is essential in the clotting of blood. A deficiency of vitamin K lowers the concentration of prothrombin, a substance involved in forming the clots that stop bleeding. The vitamin is present in a wide variety of vegetables, as well as egg yolks, liver, and fish oils.

2-4*
Testing for Vitamin C

You can test substances to see if they contain vitamin C (ascorbic acid) by using a chemical called indophenol. Its more technical name is 2,6-dichloroindophenol—sodium salt, in case you have to buy some from a chemical supply company.

A freshly prepared solution of indophenol has a bluish color, but it turns colorless as vitamin C is added to it. You can compare the concentration of vitamin C in different liquids by adding the liquids drop by drop to a fixed amount of indophenol solution. For example, suppose it takes only two drops of liquid X to turn 10 mL of an indophenol solution colorless. If it takes six drops of liquid Y to turn an identical sample of indophenol colorless, liquid Y contains about one third as much vitamin C as liquid X.

Ask an adult to help you prepare a solution of indophenol just before you plan to test substances for ascorbic acid because indophenol deteriorates with time. **Indophenol powder**

Things you will need:
- 0.25 gram of indophenol (2,6-dichloroindophenol, sodium salt)
- water
- an adult
- 2 pairs of rubber or plastic gloves
- 2 pairs of safety glasses
- clean 2-liter plastic soda bottle
- 500 milligram (0.5 g) of vitamin C
- paper
- hammer
- cup
- clear plastic vials or medicine cups
- eyedropper
- toothpicks
- sink
- lemon
- lemon juice from concentrate
- pulp-free orange juice
- orange juice prepared from frozen concentrate
- canned orange juice
- grapefruit juice
- Kool-Aid
- Tang
- apple juice
- various reasonably clear juices that are not red or purple
- pen or pencil
- notebook
- clear soda

should not touch your skin or eyes. Therefore, you should both wear gloves and safety glasses while preparing the solution. The solution will be very dilute and far less harmful than the powder, so if any of the solution touches your skin simply rinse it off with water.

To prepare the indophenol solution that you will use, **have an adult** add 0.25 g of indophenol to 2.0 liters (2,000 mL) of water. (A clean 2-liter plastic soda bottle can hold all of the solution.) Stir or seal and shake to dissolve the solid. What is the percentage of indophenol in this solution? (Remember: 1.0 mL of water weighs 1.0 g.)

Next, crush 500 mg (0.5 g) of vitamin C. One 500-mg or two 250-mg vitamin C tablets will provide all the vitamin C you need. Place the tablet(s) on a piece of paper and strike the solid gently with a hammer. Press the particles with the hammer until you have a powder. Add the vitamin C powder to 100 mL of water in a cup. Stir until all the solid has dissolved. What is the percentage of vitamin C in this solution? You will use this solution as a standard vitamin C concentration. Other liquids that you test will be compared to this concentration of vitamin C.

Measure out 10 mL of the indophenol solution and pour it into a clear plastic vial or a medicine cup. Pour 10 mL of water into an identical vial or medicine cup. The water will serve as a control. Comparing the indophenol solution with the water will help you decide when the indophenol has become colorless.

Place the two vials or medicine cups side by side. Using an eyedropper, add one drop of the vitamin C solution to the indophenol. Then add one drop of the vitamin C solution to the vial or test tube that contains water. Use separate toothpicks to stir each solution. Has the vitamin C changed the color of the indophenol solution? Does the indophenol solution now match the color of the liquid in the vial of water? If not, continue to add the vitamin C solution one drop at a time to the indophenol and to the water. Do this until the bluish indophenol solution becomes colorless (not violet or pink, which may appear as an intermediate step) and has the same appearance as the vial or tube that contains plain water. Record the number of drops required to turn the indophenol colorless.

Rinse the vials or test tubes and the eyedropper thoroughly with water in a sink. Then repeat the test, but this time use the liquid obtained from a freshly squeezed lemon. How many drops of fresh lemon juice are required to turn the indophenol from blue to colorless? Record your results. How does the vitamin C content of the lemon juice compare with that of the vitamin C solution?

Repeat the test again using drops of lemon juice from concentrate. Record your results. How does the vitamin C content of the lemon juice from concentrate compare with that of the vitamin C solution? With that of the fresh lemon juice?

Use this experiment to test a number of other liquids for vitamin C. You might try pulp-free orange juice, orange juice prepared from a frozen concentrate, canned orange juice, grapefruit juice, Kool-Aid, Tang, apple juice, other juices that are reasonably clear, and a clear soda such as 7Up or Sprite. Which ones do you think will be good sources of vitamin C? After performing the tests, which ones do you conclude are good sources of vitamin C? Which are poor sources of vitamin C?

Make a list of the liquids you have tested in order of their vitamin C concentration starting with the most concentrated.

Exploring on Your Own

Design and conduct an experiment to find out how leaving a vitamin C-rich liquid exposed to the air affects its concentration of vitamin C. Design and conduct another experiment to see how lack of refrigeration affects the vitamin C concentration of a vitamin C-rich liquid.

Investigate how you might test for the presence of other vitamins.

3

Applying Science and Math to Food

In this chapter, you will use science and math to help you understand and use food in better ways. As you will find, food that comes in a container or package is required by law to carry a set of nutritional facts that provides valuable information. The facts may include serving size, Calories, the quantities of various nutrients such as sugar, protein, fat, vitamins, and minerals, the percentage of the daily amounts required for a balanced diet, and other information related to the specific food.

Since you need larger amounts of calcium than any other mineral, you will investigate some sources of this element. One major source of calcium is milk; consequently, you will examine in some detail the various types of milk available at stores. You will also probe the economics involved in buying food, find out how the energy requirements of warm-blooded bodies such as ours are related to the level of the activities we engage in, and determine the significance of the ratio of surface area to volume as it pertains to the processing of food. Finally, you will consider how the food consumption and diets of animals are related to their size and age.

50

3-1*
Nutritional Facts

A reprint of the "Nutrition Facts" from the back of a can of sardines in mustard sauce is presented below. To see how you can make use of this information, consider first the weight of

Things you will need:
- pen or pencil
- notebook
- calculator (optional)

the sardines. A label on the can gives the net weight in ounces (oz) as well as in grams (g). There are 28.4 g in one ounce. What net weight, in ounces, will also be listed on the can?

Daily value is the quantity of certain foods that you should eat every day—the recommended daily amount (RDA). Based on the data given on the label, what is the recommended daily amount, in milligrams (mg) and in grams (g), for sodium? For fat? For carbohydrate? For protein?

SARDINES IN MUSTARD SAUCE

Nutritional Facts	
Serving size 1 can (120 g)	
Calories 210	Calories from fat 120
	Percent of Daily Value*
Total Fat 13 g	20%
Saturated Fat 7 g	35%
Cholesterol 95 g	32%
Sodium 460 mg	19%
Total Carbohydrate 2 g	1%
Dietary Fiber 0 g	0%
Sugars 0 g	0%
Protein 22 g	44%
Vitamin A 0% • Vitamin C 0%	
Calcium 40% • Iron 40%	
*Percent daily values (DV) are based on a 2,000 Calorie diet.	

If the recommended daily amount of calcium in the diet is 1,200 mg, how much calcium, in grams, is in the sardines? If the recommended daily amount of iron in the diet is 18 mg, how much iron, in grams, is in the sardines?

According to the data given, how much energy, in Calories, can be obtained from one gram of fat? In the sardines, what percentage of the fat is saturated fat?

If a person already gets 2.5 grams of sodium per day from other foods, should he or she include a serving of sardines as a source of sodium with every lunch? Why or why not?

An active teenager's usual daily caloric intake is about 3,000 calories. What percent of a teenager's daily caloric intake can be obtained from a can of sardines in mustard sauce?

The label on an 18-oz (510-g) jar of peanut butter is given below. Based on the data on the peanut butter label:

- How many Calories are in one tablespoonful of the peanut butter?

- If you put 3 tablespoonfuls of peanut butter on a piece of bread, what fraction of your daily value of total fat has been spread on the bread? How many Calories were in the peanut butter?

- According to the label, what is the daily value of sodium in milligrams? In grams? How does it compare with the daily value of sodium that you found on the sardine label? How many tablespoonfuls of peanut butter would you have to eat to reach the daily value for sodium?

- How many tablespoonfuls of peanut butter would you have to eat to reach the daily value for total fat?

- How much of the carbohydrate in peanut butter is not sugar?

PEANUT BUTTER

Nutritional Facts	
Serving size 2 Tbsp (32 g)	
Servings Per Container about 15	
Amount Per Serving	
Calories 190	Calories from fat 130
	Percent of Daily Value*
Total Fat 16 g	25%
Saturated Fat 3 g	15%
Cholesterol 0 mg	0%
Sodium 150 mg	6%
Total Carbohydrate 7 g	2%
Dietary Fiber 2 g	8%
Sugars 3 g	
Protein 7 g	
Vitamin A 0% • Vitamin C 0%	
Calcium 0% • Niacin 20%	
Iron 2%	
*Percent daily values (DV) are based on a 2,000 Calorie diet.	

Exploring on Your Own

Examine the labels on a variety of cookies at a food store. In terms of nutritional value, which cookies would be the best ones to eat? Which ones would be the least nutritious? Explain your choices.

3-2*
Getting Your Calcium

Calcium is a major component in the minerals that make up two thirds of the weight of your bones. Without calcium you cannot build the strong bones that provide the support your body needs. Nor can you grow the teeth that allow you to bite and chew food. Doctors recommend that preteen-age and teenage people consume 1,200 to 1,500 mg (1.2 to 1.5 g) of calcium each day.

Things you will need:

• pen or pencil

• notebook

• calculator (optional)

• some of the foods listed in Table 1

As Table 1 reveals, dairy foods are one of the richest sources of calcium. Other good sources include dark green leafy vegetables such as kale, beet and turnip greens, broccoli, chard, and acorn squash. Unfortunately, some foods prevent calcium from being absorbed from the intestines. Chocolate, almonds, Swiss chard, and rhubarb contain oxalic acid, which combines with calcium to form calcium oxalate, a chemical the kidneys excrete.

Some people cannot drink milk because they are unable to digest lactose, or milk sugar. They are said to be lactose-intolerant. However, they can eat or drink lactose-free foods such as Lactaid, which contains as much calcium as milk. Other foods, such as cereal, orange juice, soybeans, and bread are often fortified with calcium. Those who follow a vegan diet (a vegetarian diet that excludes animal products such as eggs, milk, and cheese) should monitor their calcium intake regularly. Any calcium supplement should be taken in a number of small doses because the body cannot utilize more than 500 mg at a time. Furthermore, acid is needed to release the calcium so that it can be absorbed. Since stomach acid is secreted in response to food, supplements are best taken with meals.

Table 1: Foods that Contain Calcium, Their Calcium Content, and the Calories per Serving

Food Source		
Dairy	**Calcium (mg)**	**Calories**
8 ounces (1 cup) of skim milk	350	85
8 ounces (1 cup) of whole milk	350	160
1 cup of low-fat fruit yogurt	372	250
1 ounce of light cream cheese	32	70
1 ounce of cheddar cheese	200	110
1 cup of vanilla ice cream	170	360
1/2 cup of low-fat cottage cheese	70	80
Non-Dairy		
1 cup of cooked broccoli	90	50
1 cup of soybeans	180	300
1 cup of fortified orange juice	300	110
1 cup of turnip or beet greens	180	30
1 cup of white beans	130	250
1 cup of tempeh (soybean cakes)	150	330
1 tablespoon of blackstrap molasses	170	50
3 ounces of sardines (bones in)	350	190
3 ounces of canned salmon (bones in)	200	130

Advertisements may tell you that you can take antacids as a calcium supplement because they contain calcium (in the form of calcium carbonate), which is true. The calcium carbonate, however, neutralizes some of the stomach acid. Many nutritionists recommend a supplement that contains calcium citrate because it has no effect on stomach acid and is readily absorbed.

As you know from Chapter 2, vitamin D is needed to maintain the proper concentration of calcium in the body. Consequently, an adequate supply of vitamin D is essential if your bones and teeth are to receive a sufficient amount of calcium. If you spend a reasonable amount of time outdoors you probably have sufficient vitamin D, because vitamin D is made by your body when sunlight falls on your skin.

Use the information provided in Table 1 to determine how many servings of each of the following foods would be needed to meet your daily calcium requirement: (1) skim milk, (2) whole milk, (3) vanilla ice cream, (4) low-fat cottage cheese, (5) broccoli, (6) fortified orange juice, (7) soybeans, (8) beet greens, (9) sardines, (10) blackstrap molasses.

In meeting your daily calcium requirements, how many Calories would you also obtain from each of these ten foods?

Examine the labels on some of the foods listed in Table 1. For each of these foods, what fraction of your daily requirements for other nutrients would you obtain from one serving of each food?

Exploring on Your Own

Is there such a thing as too much calcium? That is, can a large excess of calcium be harmful?

Devise some diet tips that will provide a person with additional amounts of calcium.

3-3*
Milk, Low-Fat Milk, and Skim Milk

Half a century ago milk came in clear glass one-quart bottles. You could see the yellowish cream (the fatty part of the milk) at the top of the bottle. Because it was less dense than the rest of the milk, it would float on the whiter milk in the lower part of the bottle. If you wanted milk with less fat, you could pour off the cream. Many farm families would pour milk into large pans and let the cream rise to the surface. They would then skim the cream from the surface and churn it into butter.

Things you will need:

- cartons of skim (fat free), 1%, 2%, and whole milk
- 10 small, clear, plastic vials
- labels
- tap water
- eyedropper
- hot and cold tap water
- food coloring
- Sudan IV crystals
- chemical spatula
- microscope slide and coverslip
- a microscope
- pen or pencil
- notebook

Today, most milk comes in quart, half-gallon, or gallon containers made of plastic or cardboard. You can buy whole milk, which still has the cream in it, skim milk, from which the cream has been removed, or milk from which some of the cream has been removed. The cream in whole milk is not visible because it has been homogenized; that is, broken into tiny particles that stay suspended in the rest of the milk.

Volume Conversions You May Need

There are 8 fluid ounces in a cup, four cups in a quart, and four quarts in a gallon. How many ounces are there in a quart? In a gallon?

How many cups of milk does it take to fill a gallon jug?

A gallon is the same volume as 3.785 liters (L). How many cups are there in one liter? How many fluid ounces are there in one liter? How many milliliters are there in one fluid ounce?

In most stores, you can buy skim (fat-free) milk, 1% fat milk, 2% fat milk, and whole milk. Milk has a density that is approximately the same as that of water—1.0 gram per milliliter (1.0 g/mL). This means that each milliliter (mL) or cubic centimeter (cm^3) of milk weighs approximately 1.0 g.

A quart of milk contains 946 mL. How many grams of fat are in a quart of 1% milk? In a quart of 2% milk? In a quart of skim milk?

The amount of fat in whole milk depends on the breed of cow from which the milk came. The milk from jersey cows has a lot of fat; the milk from holstein cows has less fat. The milk sold in stores has about 32 g of fat per quart. If whole milk were labeled with a percent, what would it be? How does that compare with 2% milk?

A cup or glass of milk is 1/4 of a quart. How many milliliters are in a glass of milk? How much fat, in grams, is present in a glass of 1% milk? In a glass of 2% milk? In a glass of whole milk? In a gallon of whole milk?

Examine the nutrition facts on the labels of each kind of milk. How does the percentage of fat in milk affect its sodium content? Its sugar content? Its protein content? Its fiber content? Its mineral content? Its cholesterol content?

How much fortified milk should you drink each day to obtain your daily requirement of vitamin A? Of vitamin C? Of vitamin D? Of calcium? Does the percentage of fat in milk affect the ratio of total fat to saturated fat? What nutrition facts change when you buy fortified milk?

Milk and Water Densities

Earlier you read that the density of milk is approximately the same as the density of water; that is, each milliliter weighs approximately 1.0 g. To see whether the density of milk is slightly more, slightly less, or equal to the density of water, you can do a simple experiment. Place small samples of whole, 2%, 1%, and fat-free milk in small, clear, plastic vials. Label the vials in some way so you can identify each milk sample. Nearly fill an equal number of vials with tap water. Place them near the samples of milk. Leave the liquids for about an hour so that they all reach room temperature.

Now you are ready to compare densities. With an eyedropper remove some whole milk from its vial. Carefully place the tip of the eyedropper in the center of a vial of water, as shown in Figure 8. *Very gently* squeeze the bulb of the eyedropper so that a small amount of milk emerges from the end of the eyedropper. Does the drop of milk fall, ascend, or remain in place as it comes out of the eyedropper into the water? What does this tell you about its density as compared to the density of water?

Repeat the experiment for 2%, 1%, and fat-free milk. How does the density of each milk sample compare with the density of water?

To see why the temperatures of the milk and water should be the same, pour some cold tap water into a clear vial. Add a drop or

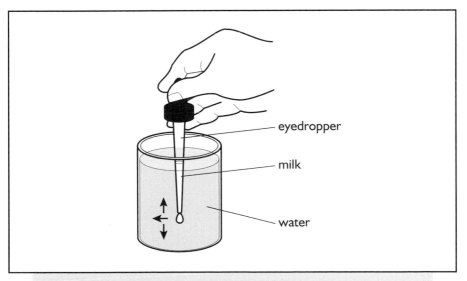

Figure 8. What happens when you gently squeeze a drop of milk into clear water? Does the drop sink, rise to the surface, or remain in the middle of the water?

two of food coloring to a second vial before you fill it with hot tap water. Remove some of the colored hot water with an eyedropper. Carefully place the end of the eyedropper in the cold water and *very gently* squeeze a little of the colored hot water into the center of the cold water. Does the colored hot water sink or rise in the cold water?

Repeat the experiment, but this time add food coloring to the cold water. If you gently squeeze a drop or two of the colored cold water into a vial of colorless hot water, do you think the cold water will sink or rise in the hot water? Try it! Were you right?

A Microscopic Comparison of Milk Fat

A red dye known as Sudan IV is very soluble in fat but much less so in water. Half fill a clear vial or test tube with water. Use a chemical spatula to add four or five Sudan IV crystals to the water. Seal the vial or tube and shake it.

Using a clean eyedropper, add 30 drops of whole milk to the water. Again, cover the vessel and shake it to thoroughly mix milk and water. Using a clean eyedropper, place one drop of the milk-water mixture on a microscope slide. Place a coverslip over the drop, and examine the liquid under the low-power objective lens of a microscope. You should be able to see tiny red-stained droplets of milk fat. Count the number of red droplets that you find in the field visible under your microscope. Count the number seen in five different fields and determine the average number of fat droplets per field. Record this number.

Next, repeat the experiment three more times using 2%, 1%, and fat-free milk. How do the number of fat droplets in each type of milk compare? Is fat-free milk, or skim milk, really free of fat? Does 2% milk have twice as many fat droplets as 1% milk?

Predict what you will find if you repeat the experiment using cream. Were you right?

Exploring on Your Own

Design and carry out an experiment to compare the actual densities, in grams per milliliter, of milk with different fat percentages. What do you find?

To prepare milk without fat, farmers used to let the cream (the fatty part of the milk) rise to the surface of the milk. They would then skim off the cream. Hence the name "skim milk." How do modern dairies control the amount of fat in the milk they sell?

3-4*
Milk and a Hot Dog

Things you will need:

• 2% milk

• package of beef hot dogs

• package of hot dog rolls

• calculator (optional)

Suppose you decide to have a glass of 2% milk and a beef hot dog with a roll. Read the labels on all three foods. How many Calories are provided by the milk? By the hot dog? By the roll? What percentage of the Calories from each food are from fat? What is the total number of Calories from fat? What percentage of the Calories in this simple meal are from fat?

How much calcium will you obtain from the milk? From the hot dog? From the roll?

Would you consider a glass of milk, a hot dog, and a roll a nutritious meal? Explain why or why not.

Exploring on Your Own

What is the origin of the hot dog? Is a hot dog different from a frankfurter?

What is the origin of the hamburger?

3-5
Buying Food Economically

Is it more economical to buy large rather than small quantities of food? To find out, when you go grocery shopping read the price per unit labels posted under the items. Cost per unit measure can be expressed as

Things you will need:

- calculator
- pen or pencil
- notebook
- food store

cents per ounce (¢/oz), dollars per pound ($/lb), cents per pint (¢/pt), or any other cost per unit weight or volume. In small stores the price per unit may be missing. Even in large stores, they may be incomplete or inaccurate. It is worthwhile to check out the cost per unit weight or volume before you buy any item. If you take a small hand calculator to the store, you can quickly find and compare the cost per unit measure of the groceries you buy.

Go to a food store and find several products that are sold in different sizes. Be sure that each item is identical in every way except size—same brand, description, nutrition facts, etc. Canned goods and breakfast cereals are good items with which to start.

Calculate the cost per unit weight or volume for each item. For example, if 15 ounces of shredded wheat cost $1.99, the cost per ounce is $1.99 ÷ 15 oz = $0.133/oz or 13.3¢/oz. Can you reach any conclusion regarding the size of a particular item and its cost per unit weight or volume? Why do you think cost per unit measure varies as it does with the size of the package? Can you find any products in which the cost per unit weight or volume does not vary with size? If you can, can you explain why it does not vary?

Food and Warm-Blooded Animals

Humans, like all mammals and birds, are warm-blooded. This means that we maintain a nearly constant body temperature whether our surroundings are warm or cold. Normal human body temperature is about 37°C (98.6°F). In order to keep our bodies warm, some of the food we eat is changed to heat. As Table 2 reveals, we burn food even when we are sleeping. Just to stay warm and keep our body "engines" idling requires about 65 Calories of energy every hour.

Table 2: Energy Produced per Hour by the Average Person Under Different Conditions

Condition	Energy generated (Cal/h)
sleeping	65
reclining	78
sitting at rest	100
studying	100–200
light work or exercise:	
walking slowly (2 mph)	200
walking fast (4 mph)	350
cycling slowly (5 mph)	250
dancing	200–400
yardwork	200–400
housework	200–400
moderate work or exercise:	
tennis	400–500
cycling (moderate, 10 mph)	450
swimming (breast/backstroke)	300–600
heavy work or exercise:	
swimming (crawl)	700–900
skiing	600–700
jogging	600
running	800–1,000

One of the fundamental laws of science is that heat flows from warmer objects to cooler ones. Because our bodies are usually warmer than our surroundings, we are constantly losing heat that, like a house in winter, must be replaced by burning fuel. In a house, the fuel may be gas, electricity, or fuel oil. In our bodies, the fuel is the food we eat. Heat flows from a building through its surface—its walls and ceilings—to the outside air. Heat flows from our bodies through our skin, which is in contact with the air that surrounds us. The more surface area a person has, the more heat he or she will lose per hour.

Surface Area, Heat Loss, and Chewing

Surface Area and Heat Loss

How is the heat that you lose to the cooler air around you related to the surface area of your body? To find out, you can do an experiment to see how heat loss is related to surface area. You will need a thermometer, hot water, and two containers with very different size surface areas. Two plastic cylinders, one shaped like a pancake and one like a regular cylinder, will serve nicely.

Use a graduated cylinder or metric measuring cup to measure out 100 mL of hot tap water—50°C (120°F) or greater. [A milliliter (mL) and a cubic centimeter (cm^3), the unit used to measure the volume of solids, are equal.] Pour the hot water into the pancake-shaped cylinder. When the water temperature reaches 45°C, or 110°F, begin timing. Record how long it takes the water to cool to 40°C, or to 100°F.

Things you will need:

- thermometer
- hot and cold tap water
- 2 cylindrical containers: one with a pancake shape (large diameter), one with a regular cylindrical shape (smaller diameter)
- graduated cylinder or metric measuring cup
- clock or watch with a second hand or mode
- ruler
- calculator (optional)
- pen or pencil
- notebook
- 2-cm clay cube
- ruler
- pocket knife
- sugar cubes
- paper
- 2 identical drinking glasses
- spoons

Repeat the experiment with the same volume of hot water in the regular-shaped cylinder. How do the times for the water to fall through the same temperature range (and, therefore, lose the same quantity of heat) compare? In which container does the water temperature fall faster? In which container does the water lose heat faster? What is the rate of heat loss from the water, in calories (small calories) per minute, for each of the two containers?

To find out how the surface areas of the water in the two containers compare, place both containers on a level surface. Then measure the diameter of each container and the depth of the water in it. Use your measurements to calculate the surface areas of the two samples of hot water (see Figure 9).

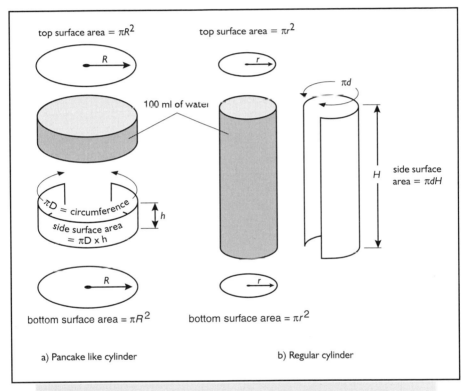

Figure 9. The surface area of a cylinder, whether pancake-shaped (a) or regular (b), is equal to the sum of the areas of two circles (top and bottom surfaces) and the area of the side. The side of any cylinder, if opened and laid flat, is a rectangle. The length of the rectangle is the circumference of the cylinder (π x diameter); its width is the height of the cylinder (in this experiment, the depth of the water). The area of the side is, therefore, circumference x height, or π x diameter x height (πDh). The total area is $\pi Dh + 2\pi r^2$ or $\pi Dh + \dfrac{\pi D^2}{2}$.

How does the ratio of the rate of heat loss from the two samples of hot water compare with the ratio of their surface areas? If they are nearly the same, then:

$$\frac{\text{Surface area of pancake water cylinder}}{\text{Surface area of regular water cylinder}} = \frac{\text{rate of heat loss from water pancake}}{\text{rate of heat loss from regular water cylinder}}$$

If the ratios are the same, or very nearly so, you can conclude that the rate of heat loss is proportional to the surface area through which the heat is lost. This means that doubling the surface area doubles the rate at which heat is lost. Of course, there are experimental errors, so you cannot expect the ratios to be exactly the same. What are some of those experimental errors?

Use your measurements of diameter and water depth for the two cylinders to confirm that both cylinders contained 100 mL, or 100 cm^3, of water.

Surface Area and Chewing

You have probably been told many times to chew your food thoroughly. Is there any reason for doing so?

Consider what happens to the surface area of food when you chew it. As a model, make a clay cube that is 2 cm on a side. What is the volume of your cube? What is its total surface area? Record your data.

Now use a pocket knife to cut the cube into cubes that are 1 cm on a side. How many cubes do you have now? What is the total volume of all the little cubes? What is the total surface area of all the little cubes? What has happened to the total surface area of the clay after you cut it into smaller cubes? How does the surface area-to-volume ratio of one of the smaller (1 cm) cubes compare with that of the larger (2 cm) cube?

Suppose you chew a cube of food that is 2 cm on a side into cubes that are 0.5 cm on a side. What have you done to the total surface area of the food? How many times as much surface is exposed to the enzymes that bring about digestion?

Food has to be dissolved before it can pass through cell walls and reach the bloodstream. To see how surface area affects the rate at which food dissolves, you can use two identical sugar cubes. Place one sugar cube on a piece of paper and break it into granules. Then have a friend drop a whole sugar cube into a glass of water at the same time you pour the granulated sugar into an identical glass of water. (Both glasses should contain the same volume of water at the same temperature.) Stir both glasses of water at the same rate mwith identical spoons. Which sugar dissolves faster? Can you explain why? What is another reason for chewing food thoroughly?

3-7*
Weight and Surface Area

J. B. S. Haldane was a famous biologist who once wrote an essay entitled "On Being the Right Size." In the essay, he noted that large animals are not simply blown-up versions of smaller animals. An elephant, for example, is much heavier than a gazelle. Because the strength of a bone, like the strength of a rope or wire, depends on its cross-sectional area, the legs of an elephant are much thicker per pound of body weight than those of the slender gazelle. The largest of all animals, the blue whale, can grow to a huge size (more than 100 tons) because its body is supported by the seawater in which it lives. On land, its lungs would collapse from its own weight.

Things you will need:
- clay
- ruler
- pen or pencil
- notebook
- calculator (optional)

To see how the ratio of surface area to volume changes with an animal's size, you can make a simplifying assumption. And, since most animals have about the same density (weight per volume), we can consider volume instead of weight. Assume that animals are shaped like cubes. Then make 3 cubes of different size from clay. Make a cube that is 1 cm on a side, another that is 2 cm on a side, and a third that is 4 cm on a side.

Make a data table in which you record the total surface area (remember, a cube has six sides) and volume of each cube. (The volume of a cube is its length cubed, or l x l x l.) Then calculate the ratio of surface area to volume for each cube.

What happens to the ratio of the surface area to volume when the length of a cube is doubled?

What is the surface area to volume ratio of a cube ten centimeters on a side? One meter on a side? What happens to the surface area to volume ratio when the length of a cube increases by a factor of ten?

Haldane also said that small animals cannot live in cold climates. How are the results of this experiment related to his claim that small animals cannot live in cold climates?

You might think that a mouse with a weight and volume about one-thousandth as much as yours would require one-thousandth as much food. You would be right if the mouse also had one-thousandth as much surface area through which it can lose heat—heat that has to be replaced by burning food. But is the surface area of a mouse one-thousandth the size of yours? Using your assumption about cube-shaped animals, calculate the ratio of the mouse's surface area to yours. In terms of food needed per pound of body weight, how much would a mouse's food consumption compare with yours?

Exploring on Your Own

What implications does Experiment 3-7 have for people who are obese?

Find a way to measure a person's surface area.

Is there a formula that will enable you to find the approximate surface area of a person's body if you know that person's height and weight?

3-8*
How Much Do Different Animals Eat?

Table 3 shows how much food is eaten each day by a number of different animals, listed primarily by their body weight from heaviest to lightest. The fourth column shows the kind of food they eat.

Things you will need:

- calculator (optional)
- pen or pencil
- notebook

As you would expect, large animals eat more than small animals. But do they eat more per pound of body weight? To find out, on a separate sheet of paper, complete the last column, for which you need to calculate the amount of food eaten *per pound* of body weight. For example, the average giraffe, which weighs a ton (2,000 pounds), eats 36 pounds of hay and vegetables each day. The food it eats per pound of body weight is, therefore:

36 lbs ÷ 2,000 lbs of body weight = 0.018 lb of food/lb of body weight.

How does the amount of food eaten per pound of body weight compare for large and small animals? Can you explain why? Do young animals eat more per pound of body weight than older animals? Can you explain why or why not?

Does the kind of food eaten have any effect on the food eaten per pound of body weight? For example, do meat-eating animals eat less per pound of body weight than plant eaters? If they do, can you offer an explanation?

Does an animal's activity level affect the amount of food it eats? Why do pelicans eat so much?

Do birds eat more per pound of body weight than mammals? If so, why? Can you explain why reptiles (python and alligator) eat so little per pound of body weight? Hint: How do reptiles keep their bodies warm?

Table 3: The Approximate Average Weights, Amount of Food Eaten, and Kind of Food Eaten for a Number of Different Animals

Animal	Weight (lbs)	Food eaten per day (lbs)	Kind of food eaten	Food eaten per pound of body weight
Blue whale	180,000	8,000	krill	
Elephant	4,700	94	hay, vegetables	
Giraffe	2,000	36	hay, vegetables	0.018
Cow (milking)	1,200	45	grain, hay	
Cow (calf)	800	22	grain, hay	
Gorilla	450	20	meat, fruit	
Lion	350	8	meat	
Alligator	300	2	meat	
Python (snake)	225	0.25	chicken	
Pig (adult)	200	8	grain	
Pig (young)	50	3	grain	
Sheep (adult)	100	3	grain, hay	
Sheep (lamb)	50	2	grain, hay	
Wolf	90	3	meat	
Penguin	32	3	fish	
Pelican	18	4	fish	
Chicken	5	0.33	grain	
Hawk	4	0.25	rodents (meat)	
Mouse	0.13	0.03	grain	

Herbivores, such as cows and sheep, eat only plants. Carnivores, such as lions and tigers, eat only meat. How would you expect the amount of food eaten by herbivores and carnivores of the same weight to compare? Why? Can you find evidence to support your hypothesis?

How much food do you eat in a day? One way to find out approximately how much you eat is to weigh the food you eat at each meal before you eat it. Then add the weights of the foods for all the meals. How much food do you eat per pound of body weight? How does the amount of food you eat per day compare with that of a mammal that weighs approximately as much as you do? (See Table 3.) How does the amount of food you eat per pound of body weight compare with that of the mammal?

If you have a pet dog or cat, find out how much your pet eats each day. Then calculate how much your pet eats per pound of body weight.

Exploring on Your Own

How is information like that in Table 3 obtained?

What are ruminants? What is unique about their digestive systems?

4

What Happens to the Food We Eat?

Most of the energy stored in food would be of no value were it not digested. Molecules of protein, fat, starch, and disaccharides are too large to pass through the membranes of the cells that line the walls of the intestines. However, enzymes produced by the salivary glands, stomach, small intestine, and pancreas break these large molecules into smaller ones that can pass through cell membranes. These smaller molecules, such as glucose, fructose, fatty acids, and amino acids, enter the bloodstream and eventually reach all the cells of our bodies.

Like gasoline in a car, food in the body is "burned" to release energy. In your body, food is "burned" in a series of steps, each releasing some energy for the body's use. For example, energy released by one of these reactions might be used to make a muscle cell contract. Like the compression or stretching of a spring, the contraction of a muscle cell requires energy.

The waste products of these chemical reactions that release energy as they take place in the body's cells are carbon dioxide and water. These waste products are excreted from the body by the lungs and kidneys (Figure 10). In the lungs, the wastes are expelled as gases when we exhale. In the kidneys, wastes, such as urea, bicarbonates, excess salts, vitamins, and water, are filtered from the blood and carried to the bladder through the ureters, a pair of tubes that connect the kidneys with the bladder. Urea is produced from the breakdown of protein, and bicarbonates are formed from the reaction of carbon dioxide with water in the blood. When the bladder becomes full, the fluid waste, urine, is excreted through the urethra.

In this chapter you will carry out experiments to see how some food is digested. You will also observe the action of digestive and other enzymes and discover ways to control the passage of food and water through membranes.

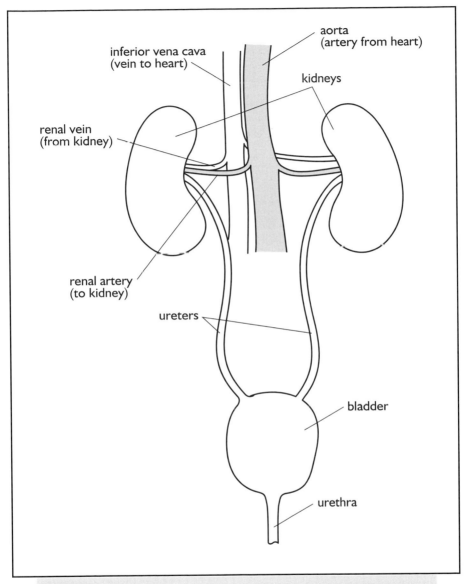

Figure 10. Fluid waste containing urea, which is a nitrogen-rich waste resulting from the breakdown of protein, together with water and excess minerals and vitamins, is produced by the kidneys and stored in the bladder.

4-1*
Digesting Starch

As you know, starch is a carbohydrate that can be identified by the addition of iodine, which causes the formation of a dark blue color. The digestion of starch begins in the mouth, where it is acted on by amylase, an enzyme found in saliva. Saliva is secreted by salivary glands found in your cheeks.

To see the action of the amylase, you will need to collect some saliva. To begin, simply let saliva collect in your mouth for a period of five minutes. Then spit the liquid into a medicine cup. How much saliva accumulated in your mouth during the five-minute period?

Next, use a clean eyedropper to place a few drops of lemon juice on your tongue. Again, measure the volume of saliva that collects during the next five minutes. How do the two volumes you collected compare? How do your salivary glands respond to the presence of food in your mouth?

To test the effect of amylase on starch, you will need to prepare a starch mixture. Do this by mixing one gram of cornstarch (about one teaspoonful) with 100 mL of water. Pour the mixture into a small cooking pan and, **under adult supervision**, bring the mixture to a boil on a stove.

While the liquid is heating, chew some sugarless gum. How will

Things you will need:
- medicine cups or vials
- eyedropper
- lemon juice
- cornstarch
- water
- an adult
- cooking pan
- stove
- sugarless gum
- small test tubes or vials
- tincture of iodine
- thermometer
- container to hold warm water
- pen or pencil
- notebook
- soda cracker
- plastic wrap

this help to provide an abundant supply of saliva? Spit the saliva you generate into a medicine cup. This is the saliva you will use to react with the starch.

Once the starch-water mixture is boiling, remove it from the stove and let it cool. Use an eyedropper to remove about 2 mL of the cooled starchy liquid and place it in a small test tube or vial. Place another 2 mL in an identical vessel. Then add about the same amount of saliva and a drop of tincture of iodine to the liquid in the first test tube. To the second test tube, add 2 mL of water and a drop of tincture of iodine. What color changes do you observe? What causes the color changes?

Be sure you can distinguish the test tube that contains saliva from the one that contains water. Then place both tubes in a water bath at body temperature ($37°C$ or $98.6°F$). What is the purpose of the tube with water, starch, and iodine?

Watch the two tubes over the next hour or two. What changes in color do you observe? What can you conclude about the effect of saliva on starch?

Another way to see the action of amylase is to look at its effect on the starch in food. To see this effect, chew a soda cracker for five minutes so that it becomes thoroughly mixed with your saliva. Spit the chewed cracker and saliva into a medicine cup.

With an eyedropper, remove a small amount of the chewed cracker and place it in another medicine cup. Then add a drop of tincture of iodine. What can you conclude? Has all the starch been digested?

Cover the cup that contains the chewed cracker and saliva with a piece of plastic wrap. After several hours test another sample of the chewed cracker and saliva with iodine. Continue to test for starch at intervals of about six hours for several days.

Is the starch eventually digested? If it is, how long did it take?

Although the digestion of starch begins in the mouth, it is completed in the intestine where amylase secreted by the pancreas changes starch to disaccharide sugars. The disaccharides, in turn, are broken into monosaccharide sugars by enzymes secreted from the glands in the wall of the small intestine. What evidence do you have from your experiments that would suggest the digestion of starch is not completed in the mouth?

Exploring on Your Own

Design and carry out an experiment to determine whether the amylase in saliva can digest starch all the way to a monosaccharide sugar such as glucose. What do you conclude?

Can you swallow food or drink through a straw when your head is lower than your stomach? If you can, how is the food moved upward from your mouth to your stomach?

4-2*
Enzymes Along the Digestive Tract

Pepsin

One of the enzymes found in your stomach is pepsin. Your stomach also secretes hydrochloric acid. Pepsin in an acidic environment will break proteins into shorter chains of amino acids called peptides. Later, in the intestine, another enzyme (trypsin) will break the peptides into individual amino acids.

To see the action of pepsin on a protein, place two small pieces of egg white from a hard-boiled egg into each of two test tubes or glass vials. To one tube or vial add 0.5 g of pepsin powder. Label this tube "P-enzyme." **Ask an adult** to pour 10 mL of dilute (1.0 molar) hydrochloric acid into both tubes or vials. Place both tubes in an incubator or small oven that will allow you

Things you will need:

- hard-boiled egg prepared with an adult's help
- knife
- 4 test tubes or glass vials
- balance
- pepsin (available from school or science supply house)
- masking tape or labels
- an adult
- dilute (1.0 molar) hydrochloric acid (probably available from school science department)
- incubator or small oven that will allow you to keep temperature at 37°C (98°F)
- graduated cylinder or metric measuring cup
- pancreatic lipase (available from school or science supply house)
- water
- 2 ml olive oil

to keep the tubes at about 37°C (98°F) for the next 48 hours. Examine both tubes at 12-hour intervals. What changes do you observe? How does the egg white in the tube with the enzyme and acid differ from the tube that contains only acid?

Lipase

Lipase is an enzyme secreted into the small intestine by the pancreas. It breaks fats and oils into fatty acids and glycerine. To see the action of lipase, add 2 mL of olive oil to each of two test tubes or glass vials. To one tube or vial add 10 mL of a saturated solution of pancreatic lipase. Label this tube "L-enzyme." Pour 10 mL of water into the other tube or vial. Place both tubes in an incubator or small oven that will allow you to keep the tubes at about 37°C (98°F) for the next 48 hours. Examine both tubes at 12-hour intervals. What changes do you observe? How does the oil in the tube with the lipase differ from the tube that contains only water?

Exploring on Your Own

What are the other digestive enzymes that act on the food you eat as it moves along your digestive tract? What is the source and role of each one?

4-3
Another Active Enzyme

Things you will need:

- knife
- ripe apple
- 4 saucers
- refrigerator
- lemon juice
- clock
- pen or pencil
- notebook

There is an enzyme known as polyphenoloxidase that is found in the cells of a ripe apple. The enzyme catalyzes (speeds up) the reaction of oxygen in the air with chemicals in the apple. Some of the products of this reaction have a dark color causing the apple to turn brown.

If you cut into an apple, the polyphenoloxidase is released from many of the apple's cells. To see how temperature and acid affect the enzyme, cut an apple into quarters. Place each quarter on a saucer. Put one apple section in a refrigerator; leave another at room temperature. Cover the remaining two sections of the quartered apple with lemon juice, which contains citric and ascorbic acid. Place one of these apple sections in a refrigerator; leave the other at room temperature.

Examine the four apple sections at 15-minute intervals over the next few hours. How does temperature affect the action of polyphenoloxidase? How does acid affect its action?

4-4
How a Catalyst Affects a Reaction

You have read that an enzyme acts as a catalyst; that is, it speeds up a reaction. Without enzymes to catalyze digestive processes, food would pass out of our bodies before it could be absorbed into our bloodstream.

To see the effect of a catalyst on a chemical reaction, pour about 10 mL of 3-percent hydrogen peroxide (H_2O_2) into a test tube or vial. If left by itself, hydrogen peroxide slowly decomposes into oxygen and water, as indicated by the chemical reaction shown below:

Things you will need:
- graduated cylinder or medicine cup
- 3-percent hydrogen peroxide solution (purchase at a local pharmacy)
- test tube or vial
- manganese dioxide (MnO_2) powder
- an adult
- chemical spatula
- wooden splint
- match

$$2H_2O_2 \rightarrow H_2O + O_2.$$

If a catalyst is added, the reaction will proceed much faster. One catalyst for this reaction is manganese dioxide (MnO_2). **Under adult supervision**, use a chemical spatula to add a pinch of manganese dioxide to the hydrogen peroxide. How does the manganese dioxide affect the rate of the reaction?

Is the gas being generated really oxygen? To find out, **under adult supervision**, repeat the experiment and then place a glowing splint into the test tube. What happens? What does this test indicate about the gas?

4-5*
Osmosis, Food, and Water

The cells of our bodies contain cytoplasm, surrounded by a semipermeable membrane. A semipermeable membrane is one through which some substances can move but not others. Part of the cause of this condition is the size of the tiny pores in the membrane. Large molecules cannot fit through the openings, while small molecules can. But by expending energy, the membranes of many living cells are able to move large molecules across membranes or prevent the passage of small molecules. This process is known as active transport.

Water, like any substance, will diffuse (move) from a region where it is highly concentrated to a region where it is less concentrated. Osmosis is the passage of water through a semipermeable membrane. If a semipermeable membrane separates regions where the concentration of water is different, the water will diffuse as expected provided the pores of the membrane are large enough.

Things you will need:
- bottle of perfume or ammonia
- vanilla extract
- uninflated balloon
- eyedropper
- twist tie
- food coloring
- vial
- water
- clock or watch
- dialysis tubing (obtain from school or science supply house)
- cup of water
- teaspoon
- cornstarch
- graduated cylinder or metric measuring cup
- 2 test tubes
- rubber bands
- tincture of iodine
- 2 small beakers or glasses
- 4 clear plastic cups
- masking tape
- marking pen
- tablespoon
- salt (kosher salt works best because it has no additives to make the water cloudy)
- carrot
- knife
- peeled baby carrots (available at most supermarkets)
- balance that can weigh to 0.1 g
- paper towels
- sugar
- ruler
- raw potatoes

Diffusion, osmosis, and active transport account for the movement of food and water between the intestines and the bloodstream.

Diffusion

Diffusion can be demonstrated quite easily. Simply open a bottle of perfume or ammonia that you have placed on a table. Stand several meters away from the bottle. You will soon be able to smell the perfume or ammonia. The particles of the liquid evaporate and move outward in all directions. Eventually, enough of them will reach your nose and you will be able to detect the odor.

Use an eyedropper to place several drops of vanilla extract in an uninflated balloon. Blow up the balloon and seal off its neck with a twist tie. Hold the balloon in your hands for several minutes. Then hold the inflated balloon near your nose. Can you smell the extract? What does this tell you?

You can also watch a liquid diffuse. Place a drop of food coloring in a vial of water. What happens to the food coloring? How long does it take before the color of the liquid is the same throughout?

Osmosis and Membranes

Place a length of dialysis tubing in a cup of water. While the tubing soaks, mix two teaspoons of cornstarch with 100 mL of water. Fill a test tube with the starch mixture. Then cover the mouth of the test tube with a piece of dialysis tubing and fasten it tightly with a rubber band. Add a few drops of tincture of iodine to some water in a small beaker or glass. Turn the test tube with the starch mixture upside down and put it in the beaker of iodine (see Figure 11).

Pour a few drops of tincture of iodine into another test tube and fill the tube with water. Again, cover the mouth of the test tube with a piece of dialysis tubing and fasten it tightly with a rubber band. Pour the rest of the starch mixture into a second beaker or glass. Invert the test tube that holds the iodine solution and place it in the beaker that holds the starch mixture.

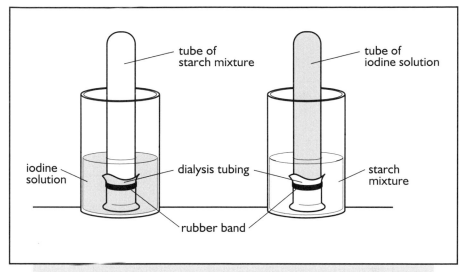

Figure 11. The drawing shows an experiment designed to find out whether starch or iodine will diffuse through dialysis tubing.

Observe the two tubes and beakers closely for a few minutes. Does the starch diffuse into the iodine solution? Does the iodine diffuse into the starch? How can you tell? What does this experiment tell you about the permeability of dialysis tubing?

Osmosis and Cell Membranes

If red blood cells are placed in water, water will pass through the cells' membranes and the cells will swell and burst. On the other hand, if the same cells are placed in a concentrated salt solution, water will diffuse out of the cells causing them to shrink.

A simple experiment will reveal the effects of osmosis and diffusion in cells. Add one cup of tap water to each of four clear plastic cups. Use masking tape and a marking pen to label the cups "0," "1," "2," and "3." To the cup labeled "1," add one tablespoon of salt. To the cup labeled "2," add two tablespoons of salt. To the cup labeled "3," add three tablespoons of salt. Add nothing to the cup labeled "0." Stir the liquids in the cups to which you added salt to dissolve the salt more quickly. To each of the four cups, add one 3-inch length of a carrot stick from a baby carrot that, **with an adult's help**, has been peeled, cut into three-inch lengths, and quartered.

Weigh a peeled baby carrot. Record its weight and place it in the cup labeled "0," the cup that contains only water. Weigh and record the weights of three more peeled baby carrots that you will add to cups "1," "2," and "3." Be sure you know the weight of the carrot added to each cup.

In which cup or cups did the carrots float? Why do you think the carrots float in one cup and not in the others? What happens to the floating carrots after several hours? Can you explain why?

Let the carrots remain in the liquids overnight. On the next day, carefully remove the carrots. Be sure you can identify which liquid each was in. Use paper towels to dry the baby carrots. Let the carrots lie on a dry paper towel for a few minutes to be sure they are thoroughly dry.

In the meantime, test the carrot sticks. How do they compare with regard to rigidity? Do some feel more limp than others? Are some easier to bend than others? Do some break more readily than others when bent? Try to explain the results you observe.

Use running tap water to rinse the carrot sticks that were in solutions containing salt. Taste these pieces of carrot. Did any salt enter the carrot cells? How can you tell? Do you have evidence that salt diffused during this experiment?

Now return to the baby carrots that you have dried. Weigh each one again. Did any of them gain weight? Did any lose weight? If you have detected changes in weight, can you explain why the weights changed? Do you have any evidence that osmosis occurred during this experiment? If so, what is the evidence?

Repeat this entire experiment using sugar in place of salt. Are the results the same? If not, how and why do you think they differ?

With an adult's help, cut three cubes, about 2.5 cm (1.0 in) on a side, from raw potatoes. Measure the dimensions of each cube as accurately as possible. Then weigh each cube. Place the three potato cubes in three labeled cups of water. Be sure you know the weight and dimensions of the cube in each cup. To the first cup add a handful of salt; to the second cup add a pinch of salt; add nothing to the third cup. Leave the cups overnight. On the next day, predict what you will find when you again measure and weigh each cube. Then, after thoroughly rinsing and drying each cube, make the measurements and weighings. Were your predictions correct?

Exploring on Your Own

Prepare a salt solution by adding 6 grams of kosher salt to 100 mL of water. Then, **under adult supervision**, use forceps and a sharp knife to remove a piece of epidermis (outer layer of tissue) from the lower surface of a leaf from a *Zebrina* (wandering Jew) or coleus plant. Place the tissue in a drop of water on a microscope slide and add a coverslip. Use a microscope to examine the cells. Note the pigment within the cells. Next, draw off the water with a piece of paper towel held at the edge of the coverslip. Then, using an eyedropper, replace the water you removed with the salt solution. Through the microscope watch what happens to the pigment. How can you explain what you observe?

Design an experiment to find out whether sugar (glucose) in corn syrup will pass through dialysis tubing. How about table sugar (sucrose)?

5

Food, Weight, and Diets

As you learned earlier, fat is one of the three basic foods that provides the human body with energy. If your food intake exceeds your energy needs, it will be stored as fat in adipose tissue. Cells that contain a lot of fat have a soft texture. Such tissue is found just beneath the skin, in bone marrow and organs, between muscle cells, and as a protective cover for internal organs. The fatty tissue beneath the skin helps to insulate the body. Fat covering internal organs, such as the kidneys and stomach, serves as a protective cushion. It acts much like the pads worn by players in contact sports.

Most of our body fat is white fat, similar to the fat you find in meat. Brown fat, which is darker and serves as a source of heat, is found in the middle of your chest and back. Some fat accumulates in arteries, particularly those in the heart and brain, where it can obstruct blood flow and cause a heart attack or stroke. Fat stored in adipose tissue is a reserve of energy that is used when our food intake is not sufficient to meet our energy needs. Fat is an efficient way to store food because it can provide more than twice as much energy per gram as carbohydrates or proteins.

Food provides the energy and matter we need to keep our bodies warm, do work, and grow new cells. Even while we sleep, the energy produced by burning food is equivalent to the energy produced by a 75-watt lightbulb. If the energy present in the food a person eats equals the energy needed to maintain his or her body, that person's weight does not change. If the energy present in the food a person eats is less than the energy needed to maintain his or her body, that person will lose weight. The extra energy his body needs will come from stored fat. If the energy present in the food a person eats exceeds the energy needed to maintain his or her body, that person will gain weight. The extra food will be stored in body cells as fat.

Aside from hormonal disorders and disease, obesity is the long-term result of eating too much food or engaging in too little exercise. What one eats is as important as the quantity of food eaten. To avoid excessive weight gain, which can lead to obesity, a person should eat no more food than is needed to meet his or her energy and growth needs. A person who wants to lose excess weight must reduce food intake, exercise more to increase the need for energy, or do both.

Energy Storage and Use in the Body

After a meal, carbohydrates are digested and a large amount of glucose sugar (a monosaccharide) enters the bloodstream and travels directly to the liver. Excess glucose is removed, converted to glycogen (a polysaccharide), and stored in liver cells. If there is more glucose than the liver can handle, it is excreted through the kidneys.

As the concentration of glucose in the blood rises, the pancreas responds by secreting the hormone insulin. Increased insulin in the blood causes most body cells to absorb glucose. In adipose tissue, the absorbed glucose is converted to fat and stored there.

As glucose is burned by the body's cells to provide energy, the concentration of glucose in the blood decreases. As the concentration of glucose in the blood drops below normal, the pancreas secretes another hormone called glucagon. Glucagon stimulates cells in the liver to convert glycogen to glucose, which tends to raise the amount of glucose in the blood. Glucagon can also cause adipose tissue to break its fat into fatty acids and glycerin, which travel to the liver where the chemicals are converted to glucose.

Nervous signals indicating hunger and satiety (fullness) originate in the hypothalamus, a small organ at the base of the brain. If the center for hunger in an animal's hypothalamus is destroyed, the animal will starve; if the center for satiety is destroyed, the animal will eat itself to obesity. It is also the hypothalamus that controls the rate of heat loss from the body. In a cold environment, it sends signals to blood vessels that divert the blood from the skin to the body's interior, thus reducing heat loss. If body temperature rises, the blood is sent to the skin to increase heat loss. Signals from the hypothalamus that lead to the pituitary and from there to the thyroid gland regulate the rate at which food is oxidized to release the heat that keeps the body warm.

Some people who are overweight produce too much insulin. As a result, the concentration of glucose in the blood is low and the hypothalamus sends hunger signals to the brain. For early humans, extra insulin was an advantage because it led them to eat in excess on those rare occasions when food was available in large quantities. These people were so physically active seeking food and shelter that obesity was not a problem. Avoiding predators while finding enough food to survive was.

Obese people may have muscle cells that resist glucose absorption and adipose tissue that is receptive to the same sugar, which is converted to fat and stored. For such people, exercise is essential even though added weight makes exercise more difficult. Exercise adds muscle cells that take more of the glucose and leave less of it available for fat cells. Of course, the added exercise must be accompanied by a diet—otherwise, the exercise may simply increase food consumption.

There are social and psychological factors that may foster obesity. Eating makes a person feel better; consequently, eating is a way to avoid dealing with other problems such as schoolwork, difficulty making friends, family strife, depression, and so on. Furthermore, social events are often followed by, or centered on, food. People who eat at a restaurant may feel they have to get their money's worth, and so they eat more food than they need. In addition, many people snack while they read or watch television, or they eat to be polite or to please whoever prepared the food.

Saying no to food is often difficult. But being overweight has many disadvantages. Fat people find that society, however wrong it may be, is predisposed to treat them unfairly. Obesity sometimes makes participation in sports difficult, or even dangerous. Added weight leads to high blood pressure, heart disease, strokes, gallstones, diabetes, damage to joints that have to support the extra weight, difficulty coping with hot weather, and presents problems for surgeons should surgery be needed.

It is clear that being overweight is unhealthy. But how can we know whether a person is overweight? And if someone is overweight, what can that person do to lose his or her excess weight? The next three experiments will help you answer these important questions.

5-1*
What Is Happening to My Weight?

To see if your weight is changing, you can weigh yourself and record your weight each day for at least a month. To be consistent, weigh yourself at the same time each day. To see why,

Things you will need:

- scale to measure your weight
- pen or pencil
- notebook

record your weight before and after eating a large meal. What happened to your weight after eating? Do an experiment to find out whether your weight changes while you sleep. If it does, can you explain why?

After a month of daily weighings, has your weight changed? If you gained weight, it may be because you are growing. If you think you are growing, have a parent carefully measure your height. Record the result and then make another measurement after another month of daily weighings. Are you growing taller as well as heavier?

What happens to your weight during spirited exercise? To find out, weigh yourself before and immediately after you have engaged in a vigorous workout for an hour or more. What happened to your weight during exercise? Can you explain why?

In the next activity you will discover objective ways of determining whether a person is underweight, overweight, or even obese.

Exploring on Your Own

Someone suggested that a person can lose weight by going to a space station, where he would be weightless. Are people really weightless in a space station or a spaceship orbiting the earth?

Another person suggested establishing a station on the moon where overweight people could go. He heard that people weigh only one-sixth as much on the moon as they do on earth. Is it true that we would weigh less on the moon? Would it help overweight people to go to the moon? Why or why not?

5-2*
Am I Overweight?

It is estimated that more than half of all Americans are overweight, and one in every four adults is obese; that is, excessively fat. In India, on the other hand, more than half the people are under-

Things you will need:

• pen or pencil

• notebook

• calculator (optional)

weight. What does this information tell us about these two countries?

Deciding whether you are overweight is not an easy task. However, there are objective ways to make such judgments. One way is to use the "body mass index," or BMI.

Calculating BMI

To find your BMI, divide your weight in pounds by the square of your height in inches, then multiply by 703. The formula for finding a person's BMI is:

$$\frac{W}{h^2} = \times\ 703 = BMI.$$

W stands for the person's weight, in pounds, and h represents the person's height, in inches. For example, if you are 5 feet (60 in) tall and weigh 100 pounds, your BMI is 19.5. The use of the formula below shows how the BMI was calculated.

$$\frac{100}{60 \times 60} = \times\ 703 = 19.5$$

What is your BMI?

As Table 4 indicates, a BMI between 19 and 25 is regarded as normal. Are you normal, overweight, or underweight? What are the BMIs of the members of your family? Of friends and classmates? Be sure to explain what you intend to do before asking any volunteers for the information needed to calculate their BMI. Some people are very sensitive about their weight, particularly if they are overweight or underweight.

Table 4: BMI Values Can Be Used to Determine Whether a Person Is Considered Normal, Underweight, or Overweight

BMI	Indication
< 19	underweight
19–25	normal
26–30	overweight
31–39	fat
> 39	obese

There are cases where a BMI can be misleading. For example, a football player might be 72 inches tall and weigh 240 pounds. What is his BMI?

Despite a BMI that indicates an overweight condition, the player's muscles and ability to run 100 yards in 10 seconds indicates that he is in better physical condition than most people. BMI is a valid indicator for most people, but muscular people or highly trained athletes may be exceptions. For such people, a better indicator is the percentage of fat in their bodies, which can be determined by finding their lean body weight (LBW).

Finding Your LBW and the Pinch Test

There is more to good health than a normal weight. As much of that weight as possible should be lean weight—muscle, not fat. You can have a normal BMI and still be flabby. To build or maintain muscle cells you have to exercise. Everyone who is healthy should exercise at least 30 minutes each day. Even a daily walk at 3–4 miles per hour for half an hour each day will help, but an hour or more of vigorous exercise is better.

A quick way to determine if a person is too fat is the pinch test. Simply pinch the flesh on the back of the person's arm as it hangs by his side. If the flesh is an inch or more thick, the person is probably overweight.

Have someone apply the pinch test to you. What does it indicate?

A more accurate assessment involves finding a person's LBW. Once a person's LBW is known, his or her percentage of body fat can be determined. Table 5 indicates percentage of body fat for different body types. Most athletes engaged in sports where endurance is important have no more than 10 percent body fat.

Table 5: Percent Body Fat for People of Various Types

Body Type	Percent Body Fat	
	Male	Female
very lean	8–10	8–11
lean	11–15	12–16
average	16–21	17–23
fat	22–25	24–28
very fat	26–30	29–34
obese	> 30	>34

An accurate determination of the percentage of fat in a human body can be obtained by weighing the individual in water, determining his volume, and calculating his density. Knowing the density of fat and nonfat tissue, the individual's fat content and LBW can be determined. However, a person's approximate LBW can be found by measuring his or her weight, in pounds, and waist, in inches. The formula used to calculate a person's LBW is:

LBW = (1.082 x weight) – (4.15 x circumference of waist) + 98.4.

Suppose the six-foot, 240-pound football player described above has a 34-inch waist. His approximate LBW would be:

$(1.082 \times 240) - (4.15 \times 34) + 98.4 = 259.7 - 141.1 + 98.4 = 217.$

Since his lean body mass is 217 and he weighs 240 pounds, his percentage of lean body weight is:

$$\frac{217}{240} = 0.90 = 90\%$$

Therefore, his body fat percentage is $100\% - 90\% = 10\%$. This tells us that despite his large weight, he is very lean.

According to the formula given above, what is your LBW? What is your percentage of body fat? What is the LBW of members of your family? Of your friends? Of your classmates? Remember: Explain what you intend to do before asking anyone for the information needed to calculate his or her LBW. Some people are very sensitive about their weight, particularly if they are overweight or underweight.

Exploring on Your Own

What advantage is there for female members of the human species to tend to have a higher percentage of body fat than the males? Hint: Generally, men are larger than women.

Distinguish between bulimia and anorexia nervosa.

Attaining a Proper BMI and LBW Through Dieting

To attain a BMI between 19 and 25 and a lean or normal body in terms of percentage of body fat, you need to exercise. Without exercise you cannot build the muscle cells that make for a lean body. By participating in sports, not riding when you can walk, not taking an elevator when you can climb stairs, and finding a job that requires physical effort, you can get the exercise you need.

At the same time, you should avoid eating large quantities of food or foods with a high-Calorie content. Also, stay away from snacks and sweets, such as candy. If the feeling of hunger becomes intense between meals, eat raw vegetables, fruit, or drink fruit juice. Eat only meals served in the kitchen or dining room. If you are overweight, obtain a diet from your doctor and eat only those foods in the prescribed amounts that appear on the diet.

Maintaining a proper diet is not an easy task. You *do* have to eat. Fasting (not eating) or bulimia (regurgitating food before it can be digested) can lead to weight loss—but such methods are dangerous because they prevent essential vitamins, minerals, and proteins from reaching the body's cells. People who are overweight need to eat food that provides all the essential nutrients while limiting the Caloric content of the food to a level less than the energy they expend. As long as the body's energy intake is less than its energy output, weight will be lost. The body will draw the extra energy it needs from fat stored in adipose tissue.

The Food Pyramid shown in Figure 12 is an attempt to show the relative quantities of the six basic types of food that you should eat. The Pyramid is based on the guide to daily food intake found in Table 6. From the Food Pyramid you can see that a nutritious diet should follow rules similar to those listed below.

• Obtain at least 10 to 15 percent of your Calorie intake from protein. For a 2,000-Calorie diet, how many of those Calories should come from protein? Since proteins provide 4 Calories per gram, how many grams of protein should you eat? How many ounces is this? (There are 28.4 grams in one ounce.) Approximately 25 g of protein are needed just to sustain life, and most diets should include a minimum of 44 g of protein per day for girls and 56 g for boys. A quart of milk will provide 32 g of protein, an egg 6 g, and a chicken breast 50 g.

Recent research indicates that the protein in soy foods, such as tofu, edamame, soy powder, tempeh, and soy sauce, can lower cholesterol levels significantly. By lowering blood

Food Pyramid

Fats, Oils, and Sweets
Minimal servings

Milk, Yogurt, &
Cheese
2–3
servings
daily
4 for children

Meat, Fish, Poultry,
Dry Beans, Nuts,
Seeds, and Eggs
2–3
servings
daily

Vegetables
3–5
servings
daily

Fruits
2–4
servings
daily

Bread, Cereal, Rice, and Pasta Group
6–11 servings daily

Figure 12. The Food Pyramid shows the types of foods and the number of daily servings of each that should make up the human diet. Why is it called a Food Pyramid?

cholesterol, people can reduce their chances of heart attacks and strokes substantially. Low cholesterol also seems to reduce a woman's chances of developing breast cancer, perhaps because it diminishes estrogen concentrations.

- Carbohydrates should provide about 60 percent of your Caloric intake. These carbohydrates should come from the complex carbohydrates (polysaccharides) found in whole grain products, such as breads and cereals, fruits, and vegetables. Avoid foods rich in plain sugar, which provides energy but no vitamins, minerals, or fiber.

- Small amounts of fat are needed to transport fat-soluble vitamins (A, D, E, and K) to cells. Saturated fats, such as butter, stick margarine, lard, mayonnaise, and the fat on meat, should be avoided because they raise cholesterol levels. Excess cholesterol can lead to the accumulation of fatty deposits in arterial walls and cause heart attacks.

- Eat foods, such as fruits, vegetables, whole-grain products, nuts, and seeds, that provide fiber.

- Most balanced diets provide all the minerals and vitamins the body needs. Two possible exceptions are calcium and iron. The growth, maintenance, and repair of teeth and bones require 1.5 g of calcium per day. As you know from Chapter 3, four glasses of milk provide this essential mineral. Since only 10–20 mg (0.01–0.02 g) of iron are required each day, most nutritious diets provide plenty of this mineral. However, iron is needed to make red blood cells; therefore, loss of blood, such as occurs during menstruation, removes iron from the body. As a result, teenage girls and women should be careful to include iron-rich foods in their diets. Liver is the best source of iron. Other good sources include shellfish, beans, peas, oat bran, Brazil nuts, corn flakes, prunes, and duck.

Table 6: Details About the Foods Found in the Food Pyramid (Figure 12).

Note: A cup (240 mL) is represented by c; a tablespoon by tbs.

Fixed	Examples	Why needed	Number of daily servings	Serving size
Breads and cereals	Breads and cereals made with whole grain or enriched flour, rice, or corn meal. These include whole-wheat bread, rice, oatmeal, muffins, and pasta	Source of B vitamins, iron, complex carbohydrates, minerals, and fiber	6–11	1 slice bread, 1/2 c. cooked cereal, 1 c. of cold cereal, 1/2 English muffin, 1/2 c. pasta
Fruits, whole or juices	Citrus fruits such as oranges and grapefruit, apples, grapes, bananas, berries, and melons	Source of vitamins A and C, carbohydrates, minerals, and fiber	2–4	1/2 c. (120 mL), 1 apple, pear, banana, orange, 1/4 melon, 1/2 grapefruit
Vegetables	potatoes, carrots, broccoli, spinach, peas, beans, leafy and raw vegetables and their juices	Source of vitamin A, minerals, carbohydrates, and fiber	3–5	3/4 c. of juice, 1/2 c. cooked or raw vegetables
Meat, fish, poultry, eggs, nuts, dry beans	Beef, fish, chicken, pork, eggs, nuts, cooked dried peas, beans, and lentils	Source of protein, B vitamins, iron, and zinc	2–3	3 oz. of cooked lean meats, 1 egg, 1/2 c. of peas, 2 tbs. of peanut butter
Milk and milk products	Milk, cheese, cottage cheese, yogurt, ice cream, frozen yogurt	Source of protein, calcium, vitamins A and D	2–3, 4 for people ages 10–18	1 c. of milk or yogurt, 1/2 c. of ice cream or cottage cheese, 1.5 oz. of cheese
Sweets, fats, and oils	Sugar, candy, syrups, jams, cookies, cakes, and pies. Butter, margarine, mayonnaise, oils, and fried foods	Carbohydrate, but complex carbohydrates in fruits and vegetables are a better source. Some fat needed for fat-soluble vitamins, but enough is present in other foods.	0	1 tbs. of corn oil

5-3*
Designing Diets

Use Table 2 in Chapter 3 to make an estimate of the energy, in Calories, that you generate in a day. Based on the estimate, design a diet that will provide all the daily energy you need. The

Things you will need:

• pen or pencil

• notebook

• calculator (optional)

diet should consist of foods that provide not only energy but all your daily requirements of protein, vitamins, and minerals as well. The food should be flavorful and there should be enough variety so that it is interesting. A good cookbook such as *Joy of Cooking*, a book on nutrition, or an almanac will contain charts that list a variety of foods and their Caloric content based on a specified serving size. Such charts also contain information about the amount of carbohydrate, protein, fat, and fiber, as well as the quantity of important minerals and vitamins that each food provides. Before you try your diet, have a doctor, dietitian, or nutritionist examine and comment on it.

With your diet and a calculator in hand, go to a supermarket. Determine the most economical way to obtain the food required to meet the requirements of the diet you designed.

Next, design a 1,200-Calorie and an 1,800-Calorie per day diet for someone (it could be you) who is overweight. The diet should provide all the daily vitamins, minerals, and protein required for good health, and it should include food that is flavorful and interesting. Furthermore, it should provide enough variety so that it is not boring.

After examining the person's daily activities, design an exercise program to accompany the diet. The exercise should cause the person to expend more energy than the food his or her diet provides. Before anyone actually tries your diet, have a doctor, dietitian, or nutritionist examine and comment on it.

If you cook your own food, be sure to follow sanitary procedures and keep leftovers refrigerated. Food poisoning due to staphylococci or salmonella bacteria can arise from people who handle food without washing their hands, from poorly washed utensils, improper storage of food, or incomplete cooking. Cream or egg sauces and salad dressings are very subject to becoming contaminated with bacteria. The same is true of hamburger, which should be thoroughly cooked before eating.

Exploring on Your Own

Do some research to show why it is important to eat a substantial and nutritious breakfast.

What is the difference among saturated, unsaturated, polyunsaturated, and monounsaturated fats? What is the difference between fats and oils?

Why is ground beef (hamburger) more likely to be a cause of food poisoning than a roast or steak?

Investigate the great variety of diets described in books and magazine articles. These might include high-protein, high-fat, low-carbohydrate, and one-food diets, as well as diet pills and diuretics. Write criticisms of these diets and discuss your analysis with a nutritionist.

What is orlistat? (It is sold under the trade name Xenical.) How would it affect the body's ability to absorb the fat-soluble vitamins? Would you advise an obese person to take it? If not, what would you suggest?

List of Suppliers

Carolina Biological Supply Co.
2700 York Road
Burlington, NC 27215
(800) 334-5551
 http://www.carolina.com

Connecticut Valley Biological Supply Co., Inc.
82 Valley Road, Box 326
Southampton, MA 01073
(800) 628-7748

Delta Education
P.O. Box 3000
Nashua, NH 03061
(800) 258-1302

Edmund Scientific Co.
60 Pearce Avenue
Tonawanda, NY 14150-6711
(800) 728-6999

Educational Innovations, Inc.
362 Main Avenue
Norwalk, CT 06851
(203) 229-0730
http://www.teachersource.com

Fisher Science Education
4500 Turnberry
Hanover Park, IL 60133
(800) 955-1177
http://www.fisheredu.com

Frey Scientific
100 Paragon Parkway
Mansfield, OH 44903
(800) 225-3739

NASCO-Modesto
4825 Stoddard Road
Modesto, CA 95352-3837
(800) 558-9595
http://www.nascofa.com

Nasco-Fort Atkinson
P.O. Box 901
Fort Atkinson, WI 53538-0901
(800) 558-9595

Sargent-Welch/VWR Scientific
P.O. Box 5229
Buffalo Grove, IL 60089-5229
(800) SAR-GENT
http://www.sargentwelch.com

Science Kit & Boreal Laboratories
P.O. Box 5003
Tonawanda, NY 14150-5003
(800) 828-7777
http://sciencekit.com

Ward's Natural Science Establishment, Inc.
P.O. Box 92912
Rochester, NY 14692-9012
(800) 962-2660
http://www.wardsci.com

Further Reading

Barr, George. *Science Research Experiments for Young People.* New York: Dover, 1989.

Bochinski, Julianne Blair. *The Complete Handbook of Science Fair Projects.* New York: John Wiley & Sons, 1996.

Bombaugh, Ruth J. *Science Fair Success, Revised and Expanded.* Springfield, N.J.: Enslow Publishers, Inc., 1999.

Cobb, Vicki. *Science Experiments You Can Eat, Revised and Updated.* New York: Harper Trophy, 1994.

Foodworks: Over 100 Science Activities and Fascinating Facts That Explore the Magic of Food. Ontario Science Centre. Reading, Mass.: Addison-Wesley, 1987.

Gardner, Robert. *Science Fair Projects—Planning, Presenting, Succeeding.* Springfield, N.J.: Enslow Publishers, Inc., 1999.

―――. *Health Science Projects About Anatomy and Physiology.* Berkeley Heights, N.J.: Enslow Publishers, Inc., 2001.

―――. *Health Science Projects About Your Senses.* Berkeley Heights, N.J.: Enslow Publishers, Inc., 2001.

Markle, Sandra. *The Young Scientist's Guide to Successful Science Projects.* New York: Lothrop, Lee, and Shepard, 1990.

Rombauer, Irma S., Marion Rombauer Becker, and Ethan Becker. *Joy of Cooking.* New York: Scribner, 1997.

Tocci, Salvatore. *How to Do a Science Fair Project, Revised Edition.* Danbury, Conn.: Franklin Watts, 1997.

VanCleave, Janice Pratt. *Janice VanCleave's Food and Nutrition for Every Kid.* New York: John Wiley & Sons, 1999.

Internet Addresses

All About Milk. <http://www.whymilk.com/milku/index.html>.

American Museum of Natural History. <http://www.amnh.org>.

Connecticut Association for Human Services. *Kids Food Cyber Club.* <http://www.kidfood.org>.

Dole Food Company, Inc. *5 A Day.* © 1999. <http://www.dole5aday.com>.

The Exploratorium. <www.exploratorium.edu>.

The Franklin Institute Science Museum. <http://www.fi.edu>.

Johnson, Doug. *Welcome to Cyber-Fair.* <http://www.isd77.k12.mn.us/resources/cf>.

Morris County Public Library. *The Food Timeline.* <http://www.gti.net/mocolib1/kid/food.html>.

University of North Carolina at Chapel Hill, School of Public Health. April 24, 1997. *Nutrition Information Source Link.* <http://www.sph.unc.edu/courses/nutr150/grplink.html>.

Index